# the Art of FORGOTTEN Things

creating
jewelry
from objects
with a past

MELANIE DOERMAN

INTERWEAVE.
interweave.com

**EDITOR** Elaine Lipson

**TECHNICAL EDITOR** Bonnie Brooks

**ART DIRECTOR** Liz Quan

**DESIGNER** Julia Boyles

**PHOTOGRAPHER** Joe Coca

**PHOTO STYLIST AND ILLUSTRATOR** Ann Sabin Swanson

**PRODUCTION** Katherine Jackson

Interweave Press LLC
201 East Fourth Street
Loveland, CO  80537-5655 USA
interweave.com

Printed in China by C&C Offset

Library of Congress Cataloging-in-Publication Data
Doerman, Melanie.
The art of forgotten things :
creating jewelry from objects with a past
/ Melanie Doerman.
pages cm
Includes bibliographical references and index.
ISBN 978-1-59668-548-2 (pbk.)
1. Jewelry making. 2. Beadwork.
3. Salvage (Waste, etc.)  I. Title.
TT212.D64 2012
739.27--dc23
2012011847

10 9 8 7 6 5 4 3 2 1

For my husband
Asbjorn Melo

And for my friends
Irene Sanchez and Heather Bejar

Your belief in me has no boundaries.

# ACKNOWLEDGMENTS

A special thank you to all the wonderful people at Interweave who had a hand in creating this book: my editor, Elaine Lipson, as well as a host of others, including Bonnie Brooks, Liz Quan, Julia Boyles, Katherine Jackson, Joe Coca, Ann Sabin Swanson, Susanne Woods, Rebecca Campbell, Mary E. KinCannon, Elisabeth Malzahn, Rachel Nedrud, Lee Craig, Jaime Guthals, Kristen Heller, Jaime Osterlund.

And thank you to Allison Korleski for seeing the value in my proposal and getting the ball rolling.

I would also like to thank all the students, friends, and bead shop owners who have encouraged and supported me over the years. It is much appreciated.

MEMORY KEEPER

MEMOIR

# *Contents*

6 **INTRODUCTION**

8 **TOOLS, MATERIALS, AND TREASURES**

18 **TECHNIQUES**

*Peyote Stitch*

20 Odd-Count Flat Peyote Stitch
22 Decrease in Odd-Count Peyote Stitch
23 Picot Edge on Peyote Stitch
24 Zippering Flat Peyote Stitch into a Tube
25 Even-Count Tubular Peyote Stitch
26 Increase in Tubular Peyote Stitch
28 Decrease in Tubular Peyote Stitch
29 Stitch in the Ditch

*Right-Angle Weave*

30 Right-Angle Weave and Embellishment
32 Join Peyote Stitch to Right-Angle Weave

*Additional Stitches*

34 Ladder Stitch
35 Beaded Fringe
36 Tubular Netting
38 Spiral Rope

*Wire and Mixed Media*

40 Basic Wire Wrap
41 Cranky Wrap
41 Opening and Closing a Jump Ring
42 Foiling
44 Sewing Snaps to Beadwork

SOUTHERN BELLE

THE STORY PENDANT

## Beaded Components

**46** Beaded Thimble
**48** Beaded Cabochon with Backstitch
and Picot Edge
**52** Ribbon Link
**54** Ribbon Strap Clasp

**56 PROJECTS**

## Necklaces

**58** Tales from the Attic
**64** The Story Pendant
**70** Sunset Boulevard
**76** Memory Keeper

**82** Dream Vessel
**88** Alter Ego
**94** Memoir
**100** Washed Ashore
**108** Fairy Shrine
**114** Lavaliere
**120** An Extra Pair of Hands
**128** Witch's Enchantment

## Bracelets

**134** La Noblesse
**140** Norwegian Summer
**148** Southern Belle

## Sidebars

**21** Technique Terminology
**75** Telling a Story
**81** Setting Up a Creative Space
**98** Keeping a Journal

**152 CONCLUSION**
**154 RESOURCES**
**158 RECOMMENDED READING**
**159 INDEX**

# → Introduction

AS A CHILD, I HAD A CIGAR BOX FILLED WITH AN ODD COLLECTION of miscellany: marbles, an old leather change purse that I had used in the first grade, three plastic bears, a wooden canoe carved by my grandfather from the branch of a tree, Cracker Jack prizes, and plastic bejeweled rings acquired from a visit to the dentist. Although most of those objects have mysteriously disappeared, I still have a penchant for collecting the odd little thing that for some reason catches my eye. My collection has changed over the years and, as in most things, returned full circle. Small plastic toys, glass marbles, and bits of broken jewelry have become as valuable to me today in my mixed-media work as they were when I was a child.

Beading attracted my attention in 1995. I began by stringing beautiful glass beads to make bracelets and earrings, but it didn't take me long to discover seed beads and weaving. After a few years of learning as many stitches as I could from books and beading magazines, I began endless experimenting to find the style that spoke to me the most. I started adding different media to my beadweaving, including polymer clay, wood, bone, and anything else I could find to help me tell a story in beads.

With the help and encouragement of friends, my teaching schedule grew. I set aside mixed media to concentrate on elaborate beaded pieces for classes, emphasizing techniques and stitch manipulation. Still, mixed media called me, and the occasional odd object began to reappear in my beadwork and projects for workshops. This book is a surrendering to something I knew I loved, yet for reasons of practicality had kept buried in the back of my mind as a beautiful silk scarf might be stuffed forlornly in a drawer waiting for a special occasion that might someday come.

When I began working on this book, more than ten years had passed since I did my first mixed-media beadweaving experiments in sculptural-themed jewelry. I started experimenting again, scouring antiques stores and junk shops, hardware stores, flea markets, and fabric shops. This book is the result. I hope you enjoy *The Art of Forgotten Things* as much as I enjoyed writing and creating it.

If you listen carefully when you veer from your chosen path, a quiet voice in the stillness will always lead you back.

*Melanie Doerman*

# Tools, MATERIALS, and treasures

**THIS CHAPTER REVIEWS** basic tools and materials for beadweaving and jewelry making. In addition, you'll find tips to help you assemble a treasure chest of objects for the mixed-media elements that make these projects so exciting to create and wear. In this book, I've aimed for materials that are easy to find and are attainable. Some are unique, such as pieces of jewelry, watches, keys, photos, or handpainted wooden pendants. As you begin to gather your own materials, you will surely find you have some unique pieces as well.

# → Beads

**THE PROJECTS IN THIS BOOK** use a variety of beads, including seed beads for beadweaving and larger beads as components. Shop at a local bead store or see the resource list on page 154 for online retailers. Project instructions include information about the specific beads.

### SEED BEADS

These are the smallest beads you'll use in these projects; they vary in size, finish, color, and shape.

*Cylinder Beads* These beads have a cylindrical shape. They have a smooth, even look when used in a stitch such as peyote stitch. I use them with size 11° seed beads in many of the projects.

*Japanese Seed Beads, Size 11°* I use Japanese seed beads rather than seed beads from the Czech Republic because they have greater uniformity and larger holes. Japanese seed beads come in a large range of colors and finishes.

*Japanese Seed Beads, Size 15°* Don't be intimidated by the small size of these beads. I love working with size 15°s—they add beautiful detail to your work. They are quite easy to work with since they have a fairly large hole. In my early years of teaching, I would begin a class by passing around a hank of antique size 24° beads from my stash. The students would look at the size 24° beads and then the size 15° beads looked huge. Everything is relative.

### CRYSTALS

I like just a bit of crystal for sparkle and use Austrian crystal beads in sizes 3mm, 4mm, and 6mm sizes. If you like to use crystals, you'll find them in a wide range of colors in many beautiful shapes—beads, spacers, and pendants.

### LARGER BEADS

Visit bead shops for pearls in many shapes, colors, and sizes, as well as beads made of pressed glass, fire-polished glass, stone, bone, coral, or crystal. Many vintage beads are available as well. Use any of these as dangles, in straps, or as embellishments on a cuff, fabric, or piece of beadwork.

# Beading Supplies

IF YOU'RE ALREADY WORKING WITH BEADS, you're likely to have many of these supplies on hand or have your own preferences for specific brands. Stock up on supplies as you prepare to work on the projects in this book so you can set your imagination free without any delays.

## NEEDLES

Have a good supply of size 12 and size 13 beading needles. I used size 12 Pony brand needles for all of the projects in this book (I also like the John James brand). I find that a size 13 needle comes in handy when several passes through a bead makes the hole too small for a size 12 needle. Though this rarely happens, it's good to be prepared.

## THREAD AND ACCESSORIES

The type of thread you use is a very personal choice. Each beader has a favorite. In my experience different threads work well for different stitches and applications, but Silamide is my favorite. Try several to find the one you like the best. In this section, I've listed just a few readily available threads available that I've used successfully. Use a thread that is a bit darker than the color of your beads. I rarely use white thread, and I prefer ivory or light beige thread, even when working with white beads.

*Silamide* Silamide is a pre-waxed nylon thread; I used this brand for all the projects in this book. I find that I use grays, black, and a mid-range brown color most frequently, though other colors are available. Because the thread has a twist, some beaders find Silamide difficult to thread through a needle.

*One-G* This nylon thread differs from Silamide because the thread is not twisted. One-G has a slick feel to it and can fray a little, especially if you have to undo some of your work.

*Nymo* Nymo brand beading thread is a nylon thread similar to One-G. Nymo thread has a tendency to fray, and some beaders favor stronger, more durable threads.

*Fireline* Fireline is a brand of braided fishing line that comes in a variety of weights or thicknesses. For beading, 4- or 6-pound test weight will suffice, with the 6-pound the more versatile weight. The 4-pound weight works well if you're using tiny size 18° or 20° antique beads. Colors of this thread are limited.

*Power-Pro* Power-Pro is a braided fishing line similar to Fireline.

*Beeswax* I use beeswax, even with thread that is already waxed, such as Silamide. I think thread behaves a little better with a coating of wax. Run the thread through the beeswax to enjoy its benefits.

*Thread Heaven* Thread Heaven is a microcrystalline thread conditioner. I don't use it with Silamide thread as it tends to make it unruly, but some Fireline users recommend it.

*Scissors or Thread Zapper*  Embroidery scissors or other small, sharp scissors allow you to clip threads close to the beadwork and end your work in a clean, professional manner. If you don't like to clip threads with scissors, Thread Zapper is the solution. It allows you to burn a thread right at the edge of the bead for a clean look. I used a pair of stork scissors for years and then switched to the Zapper.

*Bead Embroidery Foundation Fabric*  Lacy's Stiff Stuff is my preferred foundation fabric for bead embroidery, sold in 8½" × 11" (21.5 × 28 cm) sheets. Its only drawback is its bright white color, which can show between stitched-on beads. It's easy to dye with Rit dye or other all-purpose dye. I've also used concentrated liquid watercolors, or added another layer of cotton fabric over the Lacy's Stiff Stuff in a color that matches my beads. You can also color the edges with a permanent marker.

## WIRE

I made most of the projects in this book with 24-gauge wire. If the wire has to support a heavy piece, try heavier 22-gauge wire. Use sterling silver, gold-filled, gold-plated, or copper wire, or a colored copper wire product called Artistic Wire. For most of the projects in this book, I used Artistic Wire in gunmetal or vintage bronze. I match my wire to the beads in the project. Some require a warmer hue, such as the gunmetal shade of Artistic Wire or a gold-plated or gold-filled wire, while cool colors look better with silver wire. If your beads have a pronounced vintage look, try bronze colors or darkened sterling silver.

## WIREWORKING TOOLS

If you do a lot of wirework, it's probably advisable to invest in some really good tools. Don't try to raid your tool box or look for pliers in the garage—be sure to use pliers that are made for making jewelry. Following are the tools I find most useful.

*An assortment of beading threads and tools, including flat-nose pliers (left) and round-nose pliers (right).*

*E6000 adhesive, small drill, and gilder's paste.*

*Flush Cutters and Small Wire Cutters*
Flush cutters give a clean cut on wire wraps. Small wire cutters are useful when cutting the loops off of charms.

*Round-Nose Pliers*  When doing a wire wrap, I use a pair of round-nose pliers to form and then to hold the top loop.

*Flat-Nose Pliers*  I use a pair of flat-nose pliers in the basic wire wrap to wrap the wire around the bottom of the loop.

*Chain-Nose Pliers*  Chain-nose pliers have two flat jaws that come to a point, making them useful for working wire in tight places.

*File*  Use a jewelry file to smooth burrs flush to the edge of a charm after cutting off the loop.

## MISCELLANEOUS TOOLS

You'll find that these tools and materials will be helpful on your jewelry-making journey. If you've been making jewelry and working with beads, you may already have many of these.

*Double-Sided Tape*  I use a brand with a strong adhesive called Terrifically Tacky Tape in ¼" (6mm), ½" (1.3 cm), and 1" (2.5 cm) widths, depending on the project, and 2" (5 cm) wide carpet tape, available at hardware stores on large rolls.

*Glue*  Though I prefer to use double-sided tape, some components require glue; I like E6000 adhesive. I use very small amounts applied with a toothpick. I also use The Ultimate! White Glue, Diamond Glaze adhesive, and Allene's Tacky Glue.

*Gilder's Paste*  Gilder's paste is a wax-based medium that comes in several metallic finishes; I use it to highlight metal such as

natural brass filigree. It's also useful on wood, polymer clay, and other surfaces. Apply it with a soft cloth, tissue, or paper towel.

*Fabric Scissors*  For projects that use fabric, you'll need a pair of dedicated fabric scissors or shears that cut cleanly and easily. The trick to keeping your fabric scissors sharp is to never cut paper with them.

*X-Acto Knife*  For very precise cutting, I use an X-Acto knife and blade with a cork-backed metal ruler and cutting mat.

*Drill or Punch*  You should have a drill or punch for making holes in metal, such as punching a hole in the top of a metal thimble. If you don't have a flexible-shaft drilling tool, try to borrow one from a friend.

*Dremel Tool*  A Dremel tool is a flexible-shaft rotary tool with many interchangeable bits for drilling, sanding, and a host of other jobs.

*Eyelet Setter/Crop-A-Dile Tool*  I use a Crop-A-Dile tool for setting eyelets. It's not an inexpensive tool, but for me it's well worth the price; it makes eyelet setting quick and easy.

*Sewing Machine*  I use a sewing machine to make buttonholes. If you don't have a sewing machine, you can substitute snaps for buttons and buttonholes.

*Resin*  For the doming technique used in *The Story Pendant* (page 64) and *Alter Ego* (page 88), I used two-part resins such as Easy Cast and Ice Resin. I also used Diamond Glaze in the *Sunset Boulevard* project (page 70) for adhering the fabric to the chandelier pendant. Always follow the manufacturer's instructions closely when using these chemicals and follow all ventilation and safety instructions.

# → Mixed-Media Treasures

I LOVE COLLECTING UNUSUAL ITEMS, even those that some people call trash. I call them treasure, and they often find a place in my jewelry pieces. In fact, these forgotten things are the heart of my work. As you begin to collect your own treasures, use your imagination; if it can be sewn, glued, soldered, wired, or otherwise attached, then it can be used in these projects.

Start with a thorough investigation of your jewelry boxes. Broken pieces, bits of chain, pieces you no longer like to wear all have potential for mixed-media constructions. Keep your treasures organized to minimize frustration when you start to work. As you examine the treasures you already have, ask yourself how you feel about them and how you can use them in jewelry.

Maybe the broken watch sitting in your jewelry box belonged to your mother or grandmother, or an image you love was taken on a fun day with a close friend and can be featured in a locket. Perhaps you can use pieces of fabric from a favorite dress or your child's favorite dress. The elements you choose to put inside a locket, slip inside a bottle, or craft into a bracelet have the potential to enhance both the creation of and the joy in wearing of these projects. Enjoy the adventure of discovering forgotten things. Just remember not to get so caught up in giving things meaning that you never start at all.

ALTER EGO, PAGE 88

THE STORY PENDANT, PAGE 64

## THE TREASURE HUNT

Following are some of the unusual objects I've used in the projects in this book. They'll give you a good idea of things to keep your eye out for wherever you go. See Resources (page 154) for some ideas for online sources.

*Chandelier Parts*  Look for old chandeliers and chandelier parts at flea markets, antiques shops, and even some bead shops. When looking for large flat drops such as those used in the *Sunset Boulevard* necklace (page 70), choose drops with a smooth edge so you can bead around them. Pointed drops are great, as are octagonal shapes and round beads. Chandelier parts can be found at flea markets and antiques shops.

*Bottles*  I like small insulin bottles, small perfume bottles, and tube-shaped perfume sample bottles. Look for bottles at antiques shops and flea markets.

*Antique Steel Shoe Buckles*  I buy mine in antiques shops and specialty shops that carry vintage items. Try online shopping at eBay and other auction sites. Shoe buckles usually come in pairs; consider sharing the expense with a friend and do a project together.

*Lockets*  Lockets can be found at antiques shops, flea markets, bead shops, art and craft supply stores, and online.

*Photographs*  I scour antiques stores and purchase what I call "instant ancestors." I like to use original photographs in my work, but you may wish to scan and digitally manipulate

a photograph instead. I sometimes embed a photograph in resin or put it behind glass. Look for tintypes at antiques shops. Remember that you'll have no copyright worries if you use photographs you've taken yourself.

*Keys* Don't you just love old skeleton keys? Look for them at antiques shops and flea markets, along with small cabinet keys—these are a nice size for jewelry. I've also found reproduction keys at scrapbooking stores and bead shops. Some of them have fancy details not found in the originals.

## MISCELLANEOUS OBJECTS AND MATERIALS

The list at right will help you see the range of objects that you can integrate into mixed-media jewelry, and it's only the beginning. Fill your treasure box from a variety of sources, including bead shops, fabric shops, antiques shops, secondhand stores, grocery stores, toy stores, hardware stores, craft stores, yarn shops, stained-glass supply stores, and even the beach.

It truly is impossible to mention everything you could use. When you start collecting, you'll see what I mean. The possibilities are limitless.

## TREASURES TO COLLECT

- Small tins
- Match boxes
- Small brass keyholes
- Brass filigree
- Thimbles
- Metal chain
- Jewelry parts (including old bracelets to use as straps)
- Ribbon
- Fabric
- Optometrist's lenses
- Small plastic toys or prizes
- Game pieces
- Miniature cards and tarot decks
- Marbles
- Dice
- Sea glass
- Small stones
- Medals
- Dolls and doll parts
- Window screen
- Galvanized washers
- Thin craft plywood
- Acrylic paint and gesso
- Paintbrushes
- Copper foil tape
- Burnisher or bone folder
- Microscope slides
- Beveled-glass pieces
- Buttons
- Snaps
- Toggle clasps (I sometimes use only the open part)
- Silk flowers
- Paper for printing and collage materials
- Lace
- Glitter (I like to use small bottles of German glass glitter)
- Shells

# Techniques

**IN THIS SECTION,** I provide instructions for the simple beadweaving techniques that I use for the projects in this book, primarily peyote stitch and right-angle weave. If you're new to beadweaving, I encourage you to read books and take classes to learn as much as you can about other stitches. The more proficient you become, the more you will be able to achieve the beadwork you envision. Don't be afraid to make mistakes or to take your work out and redo it if it doesn't suit you—it will only add to your skill. Your patience and persistence will be rewarded with truly beautiful pieces of art to wear.

# → Peyote Stitch

**PEYOTE STITCH** is a popular and versatile beadweaving stitch with several variations. It allows you to make flat or shaped pieces of beadwork.

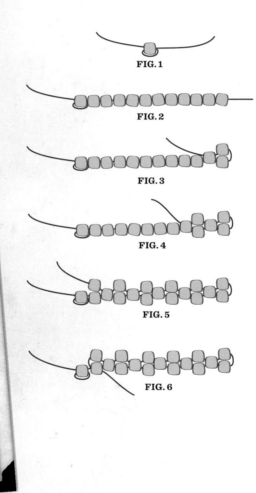

FIG. 1

FIG. 2

FIG. 3

FIG. 4

FIG. 5

FIG. 6

ODD-COUNT PEYOTE-STITCH SAMPLE

## ODD-COUNT FLAT PEYOTE STITCH

Begin by cutting and conditioning a comfortable length of thread. Thread a beading needle and put on a stop bead. A stop bead is a temporarily strung bead that provides tension and keeps the beads from sliding off the thread while starting the piece.

**1** Pass through the stop bead twice, being careful not to pierce the thread. Slide the bead to about 6" (15 cm) from the end of the thread. **FIG. 1** shows the stop bead on the thread.

**2** String 11 cylinder beads and slide them down next to the stop bead {**FIG. 2**}.

**3** String 1 bead. Skip a bead and pass through the next bead. This makes a little "T" shape on the end of the piece {**FIG. 3**}.

**4** String 1 bead, skip a bead and pass through the next bead {**FIG. 4**}.

**5** Repeat Step 4 across. When you string the last bead, note that there is no bead to pass through to anchor it {**FIG. 5**}

**6** Pass back through the first bead strung (the one next to the stop bead) {**FIG. 6**}.

## TECHNIQUE TERMINOLOGY

In these instructions, I use the terms *pass through, pass back through,* and *pass through again.*

*Pass through* means to move your needle in the same direction that the beads have been strung. *Pass back through* means to move your needle in the opposite direction. *Pass through again* means to pass through the beads again in the same directions that they have been stitched before.

**7** Turn the work over so that the bead you passed through in fig. 6 is now at the top. String one bead and pass through the next "up" bead {**FIG. 7**}.

**8** Stitch another row, stringing a bead, skipping a bead (the "down" bead) and passing through the up-beads {**FIG. 8**}.

**9** To start a new row on this end, string a bead, skip the bead on the end, and pass through the next up-bead {**FIG. 9**}.

**10** Continue stitching across the row. When you get to the end, you will have a bead strung but no place to anchor it {**FIG. 10**}.

**11** Take off the stop bead.

**12** Hold the beadwork so you are looking at the side (at the holes of the beads). Pass the needle under the thread at the side. Straighten the bead so it is sitting on top of the bead underneath it. Pass back through the new bead added {**FIG. 11**}.

**13** Repeat Steps 9 through 12 for the desired length.

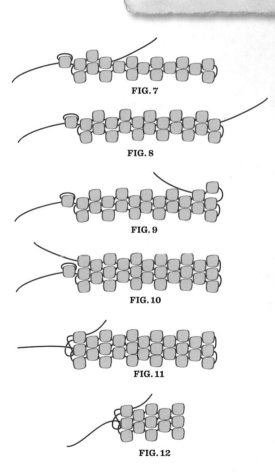

FIG. 7

FIG. 8

FIG. 9

FIG. 10

FIG. 11

FIG. 12

LAVALIERE, PAGE 114

## DECREASE IN ODD-COUNT FLAT PEYOTE STITCH

In this demonstration, I am working in peyote stitch and decreasing to a point. The start of each row will naturally decrease to a point.

**1** Begin with a section of odd-count flat peyote stitch {**FIG. 1**}.

**2** Pass the needle under the thread at the side and then pass through the first 2 beads {**FIG. 2**}.

**3** Peyote-stitch across the row. When you stitch the last bead, continue down and pass through the next bead along the edge. Pass under the thread at the side and then pass back up through all 3 beads on the side {**FIG. 3**}.

**4** Peyote-stitch across the row. When you stitch the last bead in the row, reach down and pass under the thread between the last bead stitched and the bead next to it {**FIG. 4**}.

**5** Pass back through the 2 beads in the decrease {**FIG. 5**}.

**6** Continue decreasing (as in Steps 4 and 5) until 1 bead remains {**FIG. 6**}.

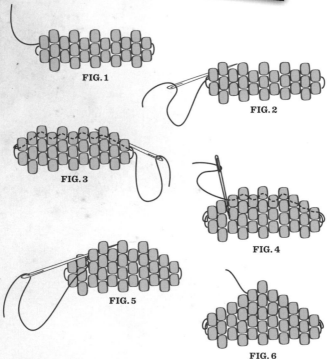

FIG. 1

FIG. 2

FIG. 3

FIG. 4

FIG. 5

FIG. 6

## PICOT EDGE ON PEYOTE STITCH

A picot edge on a strip of peyote stitch adds beautiful detail and a finished look. This picot edge is different from the one used in bead embroidery (page 48); don't confuse them. In projects made with peyote stitch using cylinder beads, I often finish the edges with picots using size 15° beads.

**1** Working in peyote stitch, bring the thread out of an edge bead.

**2** String 3 size 15° beads and pass down through the next edge bead {FIG. 1}.

**3** Pass up through the next edge bead {FIG. 2}.

**4** Repeat Steps 2 and 3 until the edge is complete {FIG. 3}.

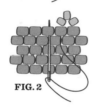

FIG. 1

FIG. 2

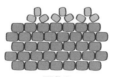

FIG. 3

MEMORY KEEPER, PAGE 76

SUNSET BOULEVARD, PAGE 70

## ZIPPERING FLAT PEYOTE STITCH INTO A TUBE

These steps demonstrate how to take a flat piece of peyote stitch and zip (or "zipper") it into a tube. It's easy and quick to do. Practice with a few grams of cylinder beads, size 12 beading needle, and beading thread of your choice.

**1** Make a piece of peyote stitch 11 beads wide and 12 rows long. Note that one end of the peyote stitch should have up-beads at the edges, and the other end should have down-beads at the edges. This is important for zippering closed. The beads should fit together like the teeth of a zipper; if they don't, add another row {**FIG. 1**}.

**2** Close the peyote-stitch rectangle and line the edge beads up like a zipper. The thread should exit the first up-bead on one side {**FIG. 2**}.

**3** Reach across and pass through the first up-bead on the other side of the peyote piece {**FIG. 3**}.

**4** Pass through the first bead again and pass through next up-bead on the other side {**FIG. 4**}.

**5** Continue up the tube, passing through the up-bead on one side and then the up-bead on the other side, zippering all the way up {**FIG. 5**}.

**6** When you get to the top of the tube, repeat the thread path that connects the 2 top beads to make sure the end is closed {**FIG. 6**}.

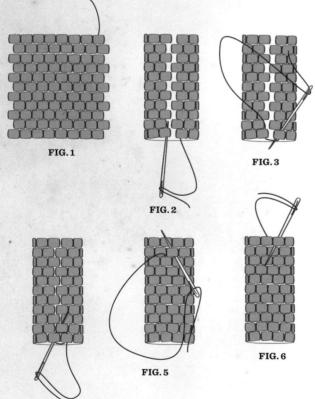

FIG. 1

FIG. 2

FIG. 3

FIG. 4

FIG. 5

FIG. 6

## EVEN-COUNT TUBULAR PEYOTE STITCH

I always use the even-count method when doing tubular peyote stitch. The rows are indeed even, while the odd-count method gives spiraled rows with one bead higher than the others. Tubular peyote stitch is good for covering objects such as thimbles, bottles, and beads and can be used with other organically shaped objects by increasing and decreasing. It's easiest to learn by beading around a support, such as a tube or stick. In addition, gather about 4 g of cylinder beads, beading thread, a size 10 beading needle, and beeswax if desired.

**1** Begin by cutting and conditioning a comfortable length of thread and threading it on a beading needle. String an even number of beads, (enough to surround the object) and tie the thread in a circle around the object you are beading. Pass through the first bead **{FIG. 1}**.

**2** String 1 bead, skip a bead, and pass through the next bead **{FIG. 2}**.

**3** Repeat Step 2 all the way around to complete the row.

**4** To start the next row, do a step-up: without putting a bead on the needle, pass through the next up-bead, which is the first bead that was added in this row **{FIG. 3}**.

**5** Continue doing as many rows as necessary, remembering to step up before you start each row.

MEMORY KEEPER, PAGE 76

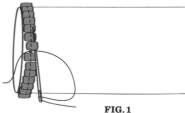

FIG. 1

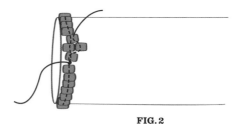

FIG. 2

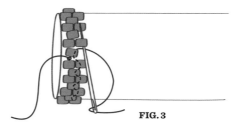

FIG. 3

**LAVALIERE, PAGE 114**

## INCREASE AND DECREASE IN TUBULAR PEYOTE STITCH

For some of the projects in this book, such as *Lavaliere* (page 114), it is important to know how to increase and decrease in tubular peyote stitch. Though the technique is not difficult, it takes practice. To practice, use a small bottle to bead around, several grams of cylinder beads, a size 12 beading needle, and beading thread of choice.

### Increase in Tubular Peyote Stitch

**1** Increase in peyote stitch when the object you are beading around becomes larger than where you started, such as at the neck of a bottle. Increase when the spaces where you put the beads become too large for just one bead. To increase at that point, put on 2 beads instead of 1 {**FIG. 1**}.

**2** In the next row, when you come to the place where you added 2 beads as 1, pass through the first bead of the pair, string 1 bead, and pass through the second bead of the pair {**FIG. 2**}. This adds another stitch and increases the circumference of the beadwork.

**3** You can cover an organic shape, such as a drop, by increasing as you go.

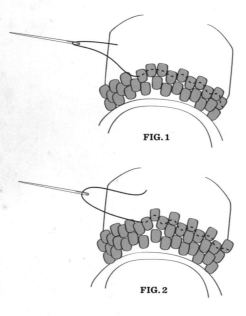

**FIG. 1**

**FIG. 2**

MEMORY KEEPER, PAGE 76

PARIS — Jardin des Tuil...

❯❯ *tips*

Always pay attention to the edge of the beadwork where it touches the object you are beading to be sure you are not increasing too much. If the beadwork starts to ruffle or balloon out and is no longer tight against the object, you may have to take out a few rows and redo them. Checking as you go ensures that you won't have to take out too many at one time.

If you need just a slight increase, instead of putting a bead in between the two, work as if the two beads are one and add a pair of beads over the two below. This is also known as two-drop peyote stitch. Knowing what to do when just takes practice.

## Decrease in Tubular Peyote Stitch

**1** When decreasing in tubular peyote stitch, you must narrow the beadwork so it will fit around an object that decreases in circumference, such as a thimble {**FIG. 1**}. To make a decrease, pass through a bead without putting a bead on.

**2** As you continue, when you get to the spot where you sewed through a bead without putting 1 on, put on 2 beads {**FIG. 2**}.

**3** When you get to this area again, put on 1 bead instead of 2 {**FIG. 3**}. This decrease is good for a slight narrowing.

**4** Sometimes you'll need to decrease quickly, such as on the flat top of the thimble {**FIG. 4**}.

**5** To make a sharp decrease, sew through a bead without putting a bead on as in **FIG. 5**, and when you get to that spot again, put on 1 bead instead of 2.

**6** In **FIG. 6**, sharp decreases allow the work to lie flat against the top of the thimble.

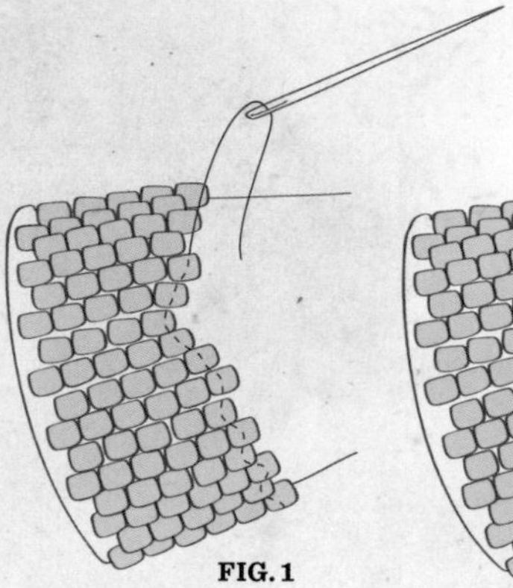

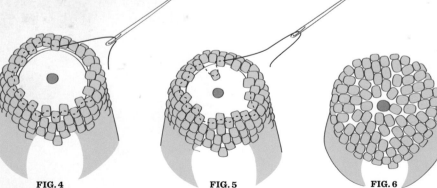

FIG. 1 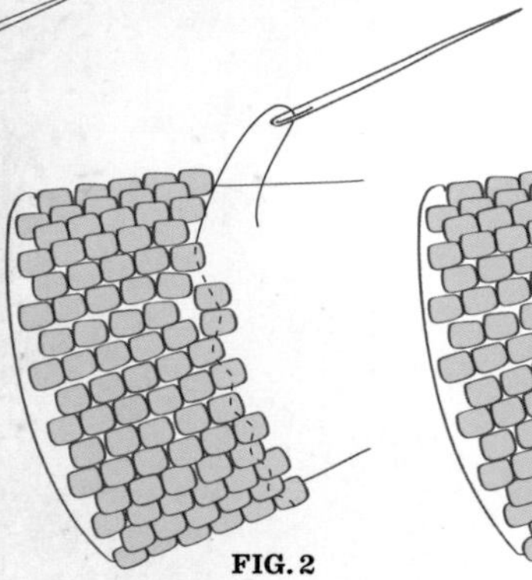     FIG. 2 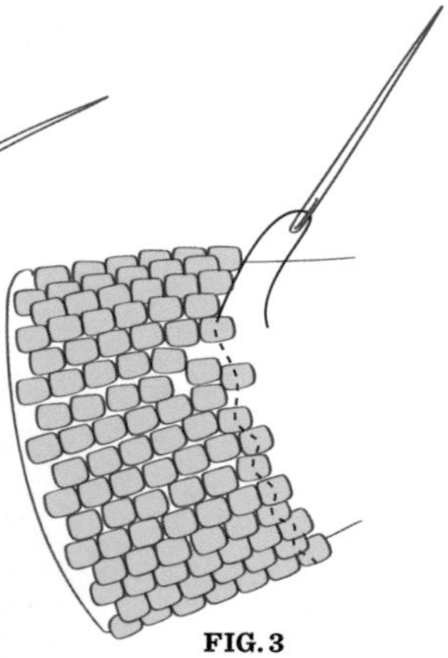     FIG. 3

FIG. 4     FIG. 5     FIG. 6

## STITCH IN THE DITCH

Stitching in the ditch is a technique used to layer peyote stitch. Instead of working a separate piece and then sewing it on, the layer is worked directly from the first one. This is not difficult, but it can be tricky to work your needle into the beads, depending on how tight your tension is. For practice, gather a piece of peyote stitch, cylinder beads, a size 12 beading needle, and beading thread.

**1** Work on a piece of peyote stitch with the thread exiting the bead where the second layer will begin {**FIG. 1**}.

**2** String 1 bead. Skip over the space of 1 bead and pass through the next bead {**FIG. 2**}.

**3** Repeat Step 2 to add a second bead.

**4** The third and last stitch is odd-count flat peyote stitch. String 1 bead. Pass under the thread next to the bead {**FIG. 3**}. The bead you add on will sit on top of this bead. Students often make the mistake of going through the bead instead of under the thread, which would make the second layer even-count and off-center.

**5** The new bead will now be sitting on top of the base beads. Pass back through the last bead added {**FIG. 4**}.

**6** In **FIG. 5**, 2 more rows are complete.

FIG. 1

FIG. 2

FIG. 3

FIG. 4

FIG. 5

WITCH'S ENCHANTMENT VARIATION, PAGE 133

# → Right-Angle Weave

**RIGHT-ANGLE WEAVE (RAW)** is a wonderful stitch that takes a little practice. I often like to add some sparkly embellishment.

SUNSET BOULEVARD, PAGE 70

## RIGHT-ANGLE WEAVE AND EMBELLISHMENT

The following instructions show both the right-angle-weave stitch and my embellishment method using 3mm beads.

To practice, gather size 11º Japanese seed beads, 24 fire-polished beads in 3mm size, your beading thread of choice, and a size 12 beading needle.

**1** Use a comfortable length of thread to string 8 seed beads, leaving a 6" to 8" (15 to 20.5 cm) tail. Pass through the first 6 beads again, pulling the thread to form a tight circle. This is the first unit of RAW {**FIG. 1**}.

**2** With the tail thread on the left and the working thread on the right, string 6 beads and then pass through the fifth and sixth beads of the first ring and the first 4 beads just added again. This is the second unit of RAW {**FIG. 2**}.

**FIG. 1**

**FIG. 2**

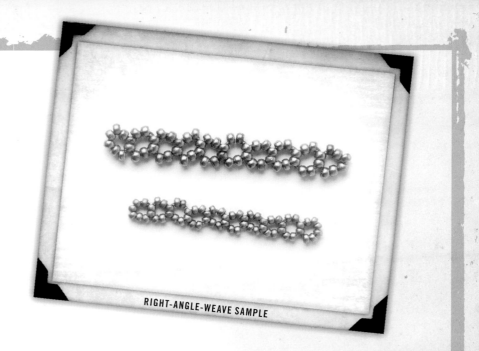

**RIGHT-ANGLE-WEAVE SAMPLE**

**3** String 6 beads and pass through the third and fourth beads added in the previous step and the first 4 beads added in this step again {**FIG. 3**}.

**4** Repeat Step 3 for your desired length. The stitch for each unit will alternate clockwise, counterclockwise {**FIG. 4**}. Our example shows 6 RAW units {**FIG. 5**}.

**5** For embellishment, string 1 seed bead, 1 3mm fire-polish bead, and 1 seed bead. Pass down through the next 2 vertical beads along the row {**FIG. 6**}.

**6** Repeat this embellishment stitch across the row.

FIG. 3

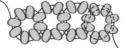

FIG. 4

FIG. 5

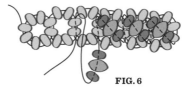

FIG. 6

➡ *tip*

Use 3mm crystals for the embellishment for a sparkly look. Avoid 4mm beads for embellishment; the beads sit up too much and place stress on the threads.

TALES FROM THE ATTIC, PAGE 58

## JOIN PEYOTE STITCH TO RIGHT-ANGLE WEAVE

Sometimes you'll find it necessary to switch from one stitch to another, as in the projects *The Story Pendant* (page 64) and *Tales from the Attic* (page 58), where the beadwork captures the focal piece by drawing in. This is easy to do by changing from right-angle weave to peyote stitch, and you get a decorative edge in the process.

**1** Working in right-angle weave, with size 11° seed beads, and 8 beads in each unit, exit the thread out of a set of 2 beads along the front edge. Using the same size 11° seed beads, string one 11° seed bead and pass through the pair of 11° beads in the next right-angle-weave unit. Continue around {**FIG. 1**}. Step up into the first bead added in this round.

**2** In the next row, switch to cylinder beads. String 2 beads, skip the pair of beads from the right-angle-weave row, and pass through the next bead added in the previous row. Repeat around, passing through each size 11° bead added in the previous row {**FIG. 2**}. Step up through the first pair of cylinder beads added in this round.

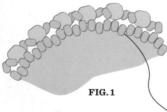

FIG. 1

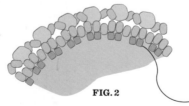

FIG. 2

**3** Change to size 15° seed beads. String 1 size 15° seed bead and pass through the next pair of cylinder beads. Repeat around and step up through the first 15° seed bead added in this round. The beadwork should close in over the edge of focal piece {**FIG. 3**}.

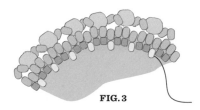

FIG. 3

THE STORY PENDANT VARIATION, PAGE 69

THE STORY PENDANT VARIATION, PAGE 69

➡ *tip*

If you're working with a very thick piece, you may need to do a few extra rows with size 11° seed beads before you switch to cylinder beads.

# Additional Stitches

I USE VARIOUS SIMPLE BEAD-STITCHING TECHNIQUES throughout the book. Practice these to expand your beadweaving vocabulary and give you more options for creative components.

TALES FROM THE ATTIC, PAGE 58

**FIG. 1**

**FIG. 2**

**FIG. 3**

**FIG. 4**

**FIG. 5**

## LADDER STITCH

Ladder stitch is a simple stitch. It's used in *Tales from the Attic* (page 58) as a loop on a link through which to attach a jump ring. This practice demonstration uses size 8° beads. Begin by cutting and conditioning a comfortable length of thread and threading a beading needle.

**1** Place 2 size 8° beads on the needle and slide toward the end, leaving a 4" to 6" (10 to 15 cm) tail. Pass through the first bead again to make a circle {**FIG. 1**}.

**2** Pass through the second bead again {**FIG. 2**}.

**3** String 1 bead and pass through the second bead again. The tip of the needle should point in the same direction as the emerging thread {**FIG. 3**}.

**4** Pass through the third bead again {**FIG. 4**}.

**5** String 1 bead and pass through the previous bead again. Pass through the new bead again. Repeat this step for the length of ladder stitch needed. **FIG. 5** shows a ladder that is 5 beads long.

## BEADED FRINGE

Beaded fringe is very simple to make and adds movement, sparkle, and texture to a piece. You'll find yourself wanting to add fringe to any number of things. Begin with a threaded beading needle and a selection of beads.

**1** For each fringe, string the beads you would like for the fringe, then 5 seed beads, a drop bead, and 5 seed beads. Pass back through the beads above the seed beads {**FIG. 1**}.

**2** Pull the thread through all beads {**FIG. 2**}. I often go through the fringe a second time for reinforcement, but be careful not to pull the thread too tightly or the fringe won't dangle properly.

**3** Repeat as desired.

LA NOBLESSE, PAGE 134

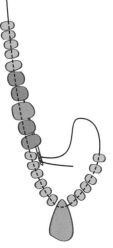

**FIG. 1**

**FIG. 2**

AN EXTRA PAIR OF HANDS, PAGE 120

## TUBULAR NETTING

Tubular netting is a beautiful stitch, textured and lacy, and is fairly quick to do. The following illustrations show the netting going straight up into a tube; if you want the netting to expand, then simply add extra beads to each row as described in Step 10. Begin working on an existing piece of tubular peyote stitch with size 15° Japanese seed beads (or start on a simple ring of beads tied in a circle).

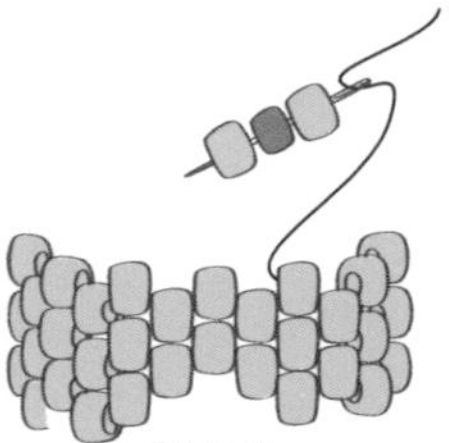

**1** Exiting an up-bead on the edge of the peyote-stitch tube, string 3 beads {**FIG. 1**}. The center bead should be a different color to make practice easier. After you learn the stitch, you can use beads that are all the same color.

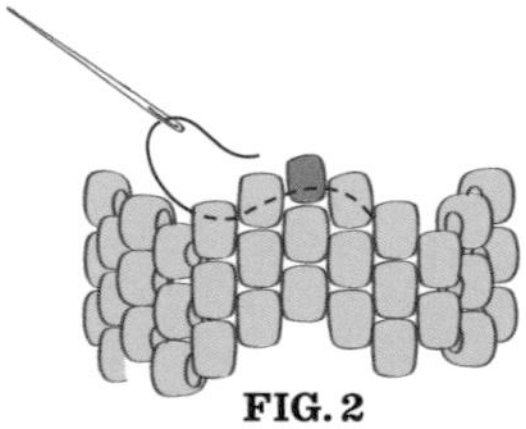

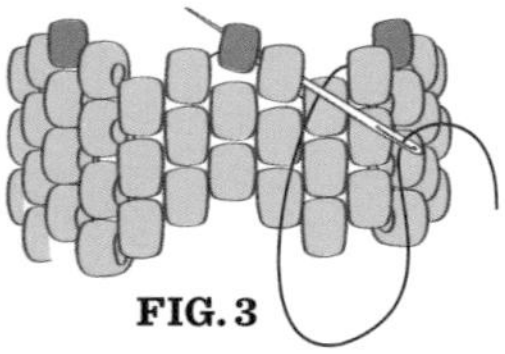

FIG. 1

**2** Skip the next up-bead and pass through the second up-bead from where your thread is exiting the tube {**FIG. 2**}.

FIG. 2

**3** Repeat Steps 1 and 2 around the tube.

**4** Before starting another row, step up by passing through the first 2 beads added in this row. The needle should be exiting from the center bead of the first stitch added in this row {**FIG. 3**}.

FIG. 3

**5** For the first stitch of the new row, string the same combination of 3 beads that was added in each stitch of the previous row. Then pass through the middle bead of the next stitch of the previous row {**FIG. 4**}. Continue this step around the row.

**6** Repeat Steps 4 and 5 to complete the next rows. Continue on until the netting is as long as you like, doing the step-up before starting each row.

**7** These instructions are written for a tube. If the diameter of the netted tube must increase, increase the number of beads in each stitch: 3 beads per stitch for the first row, 5 beads per stitch for the second row, etc.

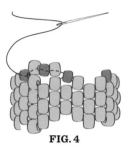

**FIG. 4**

LAVALIERE, PAGE 114

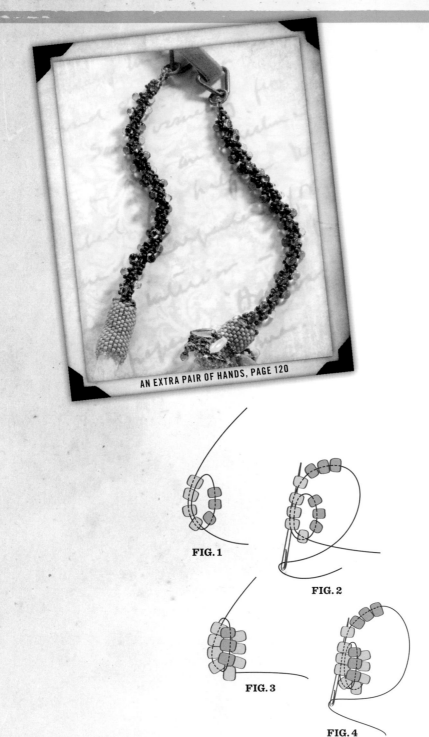

AN EXTRA PAIR OF HANDS, PAGE 120

## SPIRAL ROPE

Spiral rope is a simple stitch that makes an attractive strap for a necklace. Made with size 8° beads, it can go very quickly; using size 15° seed beads, it produces a delicate rope. To practice this fine stitch, gather size 8° seed beads in two contrasting colors (color A for the spine and color B for the spiral), a size 12 beading needle, and beading thread.

**1** String 4A and 3B and slide beads close to the end of the thread, leaving an 8" (20.5 cm) tail. Pass through the 4 A beads again {**FIG. 1**}.

**2** String 1A and 3B and slide them down next to the previous stitch. Pass up through 3A from the previous stitch and the 1A just added. You will be passing through 4B {**FIG. 2**}.

**3** Slide the second stitch down and snug it next to the first one {**FIG. 3**}.

**4** Repeat Steps 2 and 3 until your rope is the desired length.

FIG. 1

FIG. 2

FIG. 3

FIG. 4

*From top: A length of spiral rope made from size 8° seed beads with a light color for the spine and a dark color for the outside spiral beads; a length of spiral rope made from size 11° seed beads; a length of spiral rope made with size 15° Japanese seed beads.*

# Wire and Mixed Media

**THE FOLLOWING TECHNIQUES** will help you to complete the projects with snaps, wire wraps, jump rings, and foiling. None of these techniques are difficult, and a little practice will give you great results.

SUNSET BOULEVARD, PAGE 70

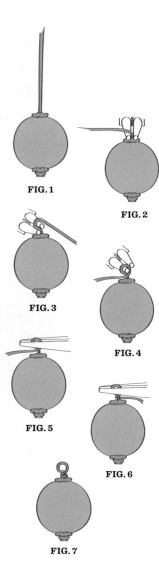

FIG. 1

FIG. 2

FIG. 3

FIG. 4

FIG. 5

FIG. 6

FIG. 7

## BASIC WIRE WRAP

You'll need a pair of round-nose pliers and a pair of flat-nose pliers to make a basic wire wrap. Practice making these whenever you can; the more you practice, the prettier your wraps will be.

**1** FIG. 1 shows a head pin threaded with a spacer, a large bead, and a spacer.

**2** With round-nose pliers, place the tip of the pliers horizontally at the top of the spacer and bend the wire to one side {FIG. 2}.

**3** Turn the pliers to an angle and bend the wire over the top jaw of the pliers, making a curve {FIG. 3}.

**4** Turn the pliers and continue to wrap the wire around one jaw of the pliers to make a loop {FIG. 4}.

**5** Hold the loop with the round-nose pliers {FIG. 5}.

**6** With flat-nose pliers, wrap the wire around and under the loop {FIG. 6}.

**7** Continue wrapping the wire until the wire is flush against the top spacer. Trim the wire using flush cutters and use the flat-nose pliers to smooth the end against the rest of the wrap {FIG. 7}.

## CRANKY WRAP

Some of the projects use what I (and my friend Irene) call a "cranky wrap." It looks as if the wire might have had a little fit, hence the name. You'll need quite a bit of extra wire. Follow the instructions for the basic wire wrap and then just keep on going. Add a seed bead here and there if you like.

**CRANKY WRAP**

## OPENING AND CLOSING A JUMP RING

Use two pairs of flat-nose pliers to open and close a jump ring. Open the ring as if you're opening a door. Do not open the ring as if you're opening a book or it will be distorted and will never close properly.

**1** FIG. 1 shows a basic jump ring that has been opened. To open a jump ring, hold each end with a pair of flat-nose pliers and turn one end away from you.

**FIG. 1**

WITCH'S ENCHANTMENT, PAGE 128

WASHED ASHORE, PAGE 100

FAIRY SHRINE, PAGE 108

## FOILING

The *Fairy Shrine* project (page 108) uses this copper-foiling technique to neatly surround the glass slide and box; in *Tales from the Attic* (page 58), it's used to surround two pieces of bezeled glass. You'll find the supplies you need online, at stained-glass-supply stores, or art-supply stores. In the illustrations that follow, I'm using ¼" (6 mm) copper-foil tape to surround two microscope slides with two photographs placed back-to-back in between the slides. My tools are scissors to cut the foil tape and a burnishing tool.

**1** As noted, the demonstration object is two microscope slides with two photographs placed back-to-back in between the slides. Begin at the center bottom of the object. Center the edge of the sandwiched glass on the tape {**FIG. 1**}.

**2** Continue applying the tape around the glass, trying to keep the glass as centered as possible {**FIG. 2**}.

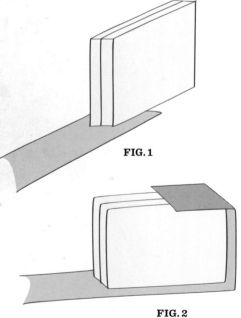

FIG. 1

FIG. 2

**3** When you reach the starting point, cut the foil with an overlap of at least ¼" (6 mm).

**4** Press the end of the tape against the bottom of the glass, keeping the edges even.

**5** Use the burnishing tool to press the edges of the tape onto one surface of the glass {**FIG. 3**}.

**6** Fold the corners of the tape over and continue around the glass.

**7** Repeat on the other surface of the glass. For a smooth look, burnish the tape all the way around on both sides with the burnishing tool {**FIG. 4**}. Be sure to burnish the tape on the edges of the glass. When the copper tape is burnished and smooth, foiling is complete.

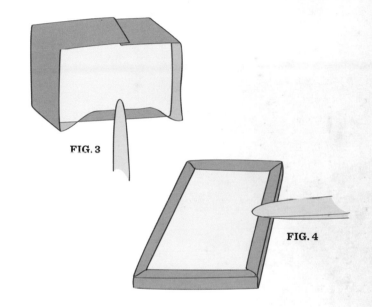

FIG. 3

FIG. 4

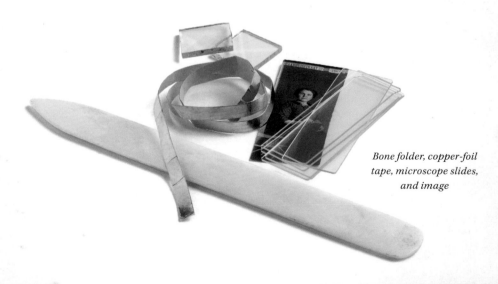

*Bone folder, copper-foil tape, microscope slides, and image*

MEMORY KEEPER, PAGE 76

## SEWING SNAPS TO BEADWORK

Sewing snaps onto beadwork can be tricky; I've had students tell me that they have a difficult time doing this neatly. There is a trick to it, and after you learn it, you'll enjoy having snaps as a closure. In this demonstration, I work with premium-quality synthetic suede fabric. You'll also need small sharp scissors, snaps to practice with, a size 12 beading needle threaded with doubled thread, and a piece of beadwork.

**1** Cut a square of fabric slightly bigger than the snap. Cut a tiny hole in the center.

**2** Place the female side of the snap with the protrusion fitting in the hole. Sew the snap onto the fabric using a doubled thread and taking several stitches through each hole in the snap {FIG. 1}.

**3** With small scissors, trim the fabric around the snap, being careful not to cut the threads. This makes a gasket for the snap so the protrusion doesn't create a bump in the beadwork.

**4** Sew the first hole in the snap closest to the edge of the beadwork (I call this the north hole). Bring the needle through the center bead {FIG. 2}.

FIG. 1

FIG. 2

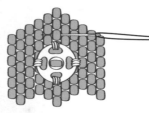

FIG. 3

**5** Bring the needle through the hole in the snap. Go through the bead again and then back through the hole in the snap.

**6** When you have brought the thread through the hole in the snap, pass it underneath the snap {**FIG. 3**}.

**7** Bring the needle up through the next hole. You are working around the snap. Bring the needle down through the beadwork near the hole. Pass the needle through a bead.

**8** Bring the needle back through the beadwork and through the hole in the snap. You may have to angle it to get it through the hole {**FIG. 4**}.

**9** When the thread is coming out of the west hole, pass the needle underneath and come out of the south hole {**FIG. 5**}.

**10** Bring the needle through a bead near the hole in the snap. Sew through the east hole as you did in Steps 7 through 9. Weave the thread into the beadwork to secure before clipping thread.

**11** Sew the male side of the snap to the beadwork in the proper spot and on the correct side. You do not need a fabric backing for this part of the snap {**FIG. 6**}.

LA NOBLESSE, PAGE 134

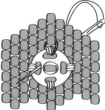

FIG. 4

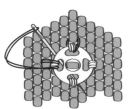

FIG. 5

FIG. 6

# Beaded Components

**I LOVE TO COMBINE** a few favorite beaded components in inventive new ways. Here are my methods for making beaded thimbles, beaded cabochons, ribbon links, and ribbon strap clasps. You'll see these elements combined in many of the projects in this book.

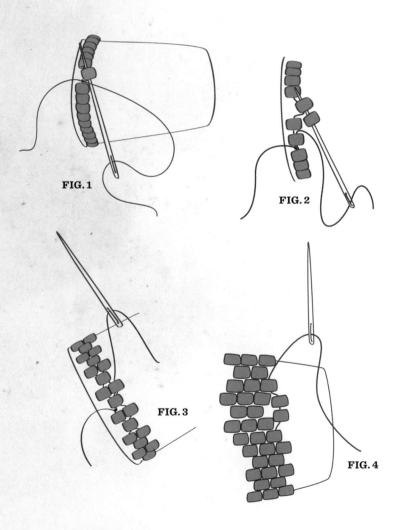

FIG. 1

FIG. 2

FIG. 3

FIG. 4

## BEADED THIMBLE

I like to bead thimbles that have a hole drilled in the top and use them as large decorative bead caps, as shown in *Memory Keeper* on page 76. If you're unable to find thimbles with holes already drilled, do it yourself with a drill that can drill metal, following all safety precautions; I use a Dremel tool with Flex Shaft attachment. To practice, in addition to a thimble with a hole drilled in the top center, you'll need Terrifically Tacky double-sided tape, 4 grams of cylinder beads per thimble, beading thread, size 12 beading needle, and a permanent marker in a color to match the beads.

**1** With a permanent marker in a color similar to the cylinder beads, color the bottom edge of the thimble. Thread the needle with a comfortable length of thread. String an even number of beads on the thread. Put a piece of double-sided tape along the bottom of the thimble, above the colored edge. Tie the beads in a circle along the bottom edge.

**2** Without adding a bead, pass your needle through the first bead and pull the thread through {**FIG. 1**}.

**3** Put a bead on the needle, skip a bead, and pass the needle through the next bead {**FIG. 2**}.

**4** Continue in this fashion all the way around the thimble. When you reach the end of the row, do a step-up: without putting a bead on the needle, pass through the first bead added in this row. You will step-up at the beginning of each row {FIG. 3}.

**5** Continue the peyote stitch until you reach the area where the thimble narrows. Begin to decrease: go through a bead without putting a bead on the needle. The number of decreases depends on the size and shape of the thimble. On a typical thimble, I make three decreases after every sixth stitch.

**6** When beading a thimble that narrows only slightly, I put on 2 beads when I arrive at the next logical place to decrease. If your thimble has a more acute shape, you may want to put on just 1 bead. Practice will help you judge the rate of decrease {FIG. 4}.

**7** The slower rate of decrease (2 beads instead of 1) prevents a large hole in the beadwork {FIG. 5}.

**8** Continue stitching in peyote stitch and decreasing as needed until the beadwork reaches slightly above top edge of the thimble.

**9** Decrease again. I decrease every third stitch at the top of the thimble for shaping.

**10** Decrease until the beadwork is close to the hole in the top of the thimble. Leave a small amount of space around the hole. Decrease sharply at this point, according to the shape of the thimble {FIG. 6}.

**11** If the beaded thimble is to be used as a bead cap, tie a knot in the threads and add a bit of glue to the knot for extra security. When the glue is dry, bend a wire under the knot and bring through the hole in the thimble. Put a larger bead on the wire at the top to take up any extra space around the edge of the beadwork and make a wire wrap on top of the bead {FIG. 7}.

**12** Bring the thread to the bottom edge and add a few more rows of peyote stitch to completely cover the edge of the thimble. Add peaks along the bottom by skipping every other stitch. The beaded thimble is complete; add embellishments if you wish.

**MEMORY KEEPER, PAGE 76**

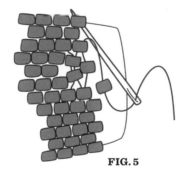

**FIG. 5**

**FIG. 6**

**FIG. 7**

SOUTHERN BELLE, PAGE 148

## BEADED CABOCHON

Not only are beaded cabochons enjoyable to create, they make a fantastic focal piece as well as a beautiful link in your mixed-media creations. There are wonderful vintage glass cabs to choose from and also a variety of stone cabs and even flat beads to use. To practice, gather a size 12 beading needle, a permanent marker to match the beads you'll use, and the following materials:

▷ Cabochon

▷ Terrifically Tacky double-sided tape

▷ Beading foundation

▷ Size 15° Japanese seed beads

▷ Synthetic suede fabric

▷ Beading thread

▷ *Optional:* Size 11° Japanese seed beads or cylinder beads, if doing more than one row

**1** Attach the cabochon to the beading foundation with double-sided tape.

**2** Cut a comfortable length of thread. Tie a knot at the end. Bring the needle and thread through the beading foundation about 1 bead space away from the edge of the cabochon {**FIG. 1**}.

**3** Using size 15° seed beads, string 3 beads and bring the needle down through the beading foundation at the end of the 3 beads {**FIG. 2**}.

**4** Bring the needle back up through the beading foundation at the beginning of the 3 beads. This is close to the knot.

FIG. 1

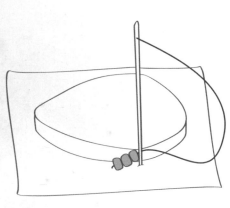

FIG. 2

**5** Pass the needle through the 3 beads again {FIG. 3}.

**6** String 3 beads. Bring the needle down through the beading foundation at the end of the 3 new beads.

**7** Bring the needle back through the beading foundation the space of 4 beads. Pass through the 4 beads again {FIG. 4}.

**8** Continue in this manner, repeating Steps 6 and 7 all around the cabochon {FIG. 5}.

**9** To make a peyote-stitched bezel around the cabochon, put a bead on the needle. Skip a bead. Pass the needle through the next bead {FIG. 6}.

**10** Continue in peyote stitch around the cabochon. When the round is finished, step up by passing through the first bead added in this round again {FIG. 7}.

**11** The first row of peyote stitch is complete, but the bezel must cover the edge to keep the stone from falling out. Continue adding rounds of peyote stitch until the bezel is slightly higher than the edge of the cabochon.

**12** The next round adds a decorative peaked edge and will tighten the bezel to hold the stone in place. Put on 1 bead as if you are starting a new row {FIG. 8}.

**13** Skip the next stitch by passing the needle through the next 2 beads without putting a bead on {FIG. 9}. Continue making peaks all around the stone.

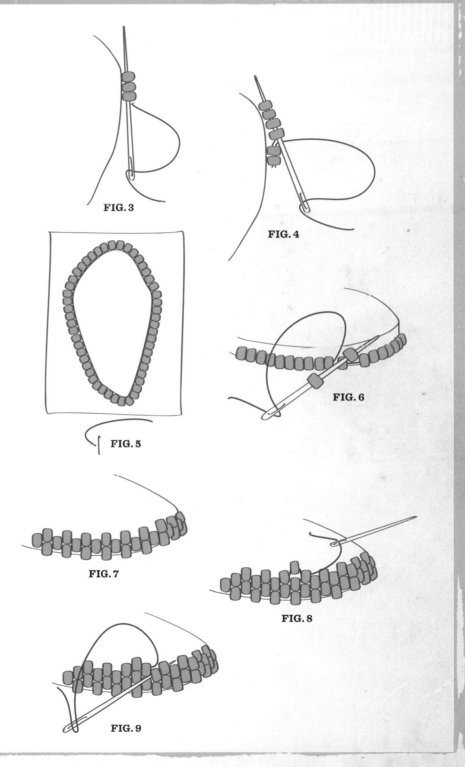

FIG. 3

FIG. 4

FIG. 5

FIG. 6

FIG. 7

FIG. 8

FIG. 9

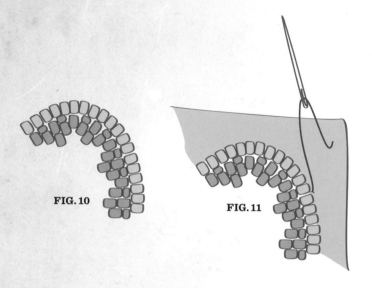

**FIG. 10**

**FIG. 11**

**14** Bring the needle up through the beading foundation 1 bead space away from the first row. Backstitch another row around the stone as in Steps 2 through 8. There is no peyote stitch on top of this row {**FIG. 10**}.

**15** Trim away the excess beading foundation (turn the cabochon over and trim from underneath so you don't cut your stitches).

**16** Attach a new thread to the edge of the beading foundation. Using double-sided tape, adhere the cabochon to a piece of synthetic suede {**FIG. 11**}.

**17** With small sharp scissors, trim the synthetic suede so it is flush with the beading foundation. Use a permanent marker to color the edge of the beading foundation.

MEMOIR, PAGE 94

## Add a Picot Edge

**18** To make a picot edge, string 3 size 15° seed beads. Bring the needle up through the synthetic suede and beading foundation about 1 bead space from where the thread is coming out {**FIG. 12**}.

**19** Pass back through the last bead strung. The needle should be pointing out from the edge {**FIG. 13**}.

**20** String 2 size 15° seed beads. Bring the needle up through the synthetic suede and beading foundation about 1 bead space from where the thread is coming out {**FIG. 14**}.

**21** Pass back through the last bead added. The needle should be pointing away from the fabric edge as you make the stitch {**FIG. 15**}.

**22** FIG. 16 illustrates an edge with several completed picots.

**23** Repeat Step 19 around and connect your last picot to the first one. You now have a finished beaded cabochon, ready to sew on a project.

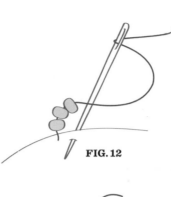

FIG. 12

FIG. 13

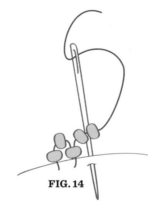

FIG. 14

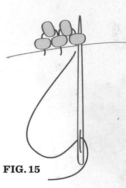

FIG. 15

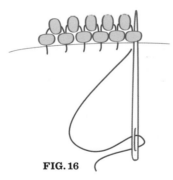

FIG. 16

AN EXTRA PAIR OF HANDS, PAGE 120

## RIBBON LINK

A ribbon link is a wonderful way to add texture and color to a design. I especially love using velvet and satin ribbons. This is one of my favorite beadwork components, and there are variations on this basic ribbon link throughout the book. To practice, use a size 12 beading needle and the following materials:

- ➤ Cylinder beads
- ➤ Size 15° Japanese seed beads
- ➤ Velvet or satin ribbon
- ➤ Large triangular or round jump ring
- ➤ 2 Japanese drops, 3.4mm
- ➤ Beading thread

**1** Stitch a piece of odd-count flat peyote stitch (page 20) as wide as the ribbon and 20 rows long (10 beads stacked up the side). Decrease each end to a point (page 22) and make a picot edge along each side (page 23). The thread will be emerging from a center bead at one end {**FIG. 1**}.

**2** Cut the ribbon and fold in half through a triangular or round jump ring {**FIG. 2**}. The ends of the ribbon will meet, wrong sides together, opposite the jump ring.

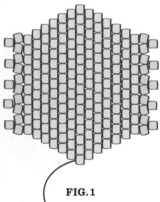

FIG. 1

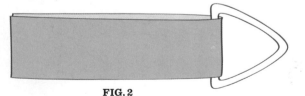

FIG. 2

**3** Fold the beadwork that you made in Step 1 over the cut edges of the ribbon and stitch through the ribbon to the center bead on the other side. Go through the center bead and reinforce. Stitch along the bottom edge of the beadwork to secure it well to the ribbon {FIG. 3}.

**4** On both sides, add a Japanese drop to the center bead with a size 15º seed bead on either side of the drop {FIG. 4}. Use the link as is, or go on to Step 5 to dress up the edge of the ribbon with a picot edge.

**5** Starting next to the beadwork, make a picot edge along the edge of the ribbon, being sure to bring the needle through both layers of ribbon. Tie off thread. To make the picot edge along the other side, begin by tying the thread in the beadwork and bring the needle and thread out between the ribbon layers near the beadwork. Work down toward the jump ring. If you stitch from the jump ring up, you may end up with a pucker near the beadwork. Using an odd number of beads, make a loop of cylinder beads at the top center of the beadwork. The link is complete.

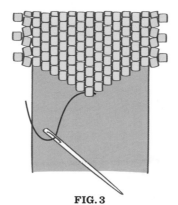

**FIG. 3**

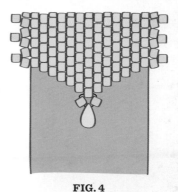

**FIG. 4**

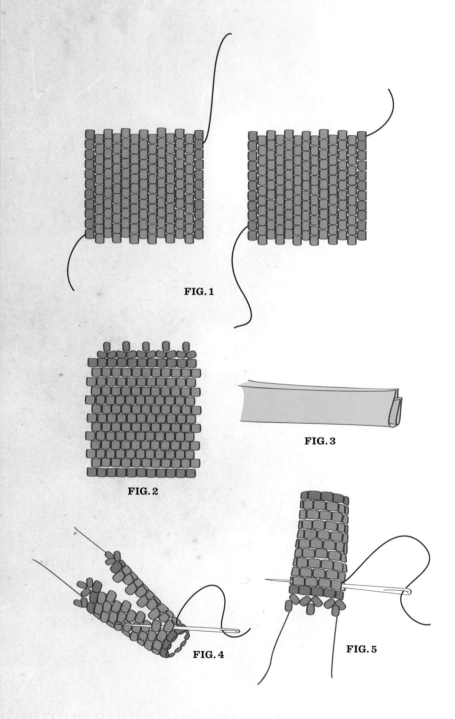

**FIG. 1**

**FIG. 2**

**FIG. 3**

**FIG. 4**

**FIG. 5**

## RIBBON STRAP CLASP

I often wrap the ends of ribbons in peyote-stitch rectangles and then attach clasps to the beadwork. It finishes the ends of the ribbon beautifully and adds strength and texture. This is my basic technique to enclose the ends of ribbon straps. To practice, use a size 12 beading needle and the following materials:

➢ Cylinder beads

➢ Size 15° Japanese seed beads

➢ Ribbon

➢ Shank-style button, ¾" (2 cm) diameter

➢ 8 fire-polished glass beads, 3mm

➢ 1 dagger bead

➢ Beading thread

**1** Make two pieces of peyote stitch that will wrap around your ribbon. In **FIG. 1**, I worked with 11 beads stacked on the edge. For a very narrow ribbon, 8 beads stacked on the edge will work well.

**2** Make picots along one edge by exiting out 1 cylinder bead, string 3 size 15° seed beads, pass back through the next cylinder bead along. Pass back out the next cylinder bead. Repeat for the length of the piece {**FIG. 2**}.

**3** Fold the ribbon tightly, as shown in **FIG. 3**. If you are using a very wide ribbon (or several fibers held together), you may want to sew the folded end together first and wrap thread around it before you zipper the peyote-stitched piece to close around it.

**4** Wrap the peyote-stitch piece around the ribbon with the picots toward the bottom. Begin to zipper it closed as described on page 24 {**FIG. 4**}.

**5** When you get to the end, start to work back up to the starting point. Bring the needle through the tube, making sure you go through the ribbon inside {FIG. 5}. Do this all the way up to secure the ribbon inside. Repeat Steps 3 through 5 on the other ribbon end.

**6** For the button closure, string 3 cylinder beads, 1 shank-style button, and 3 cylinder beads {FIG. 6}. You may wish to add more cylinders depending on the shape of the button and width of the shank.

**7** Bring the needle down into a bead on the other side of the tube {FIG. 7}. Stitch to reinforce.

**8** FIG. 8 shows the wrap and attached button.

**9** For the loop closure on the second ribbon end, string 2 cylinder beads, alternate 4 size 3mm fire-polished beads with cylinders between them, 1 dagger bead, and repeat in reverse for the second side of the closure. Before you reinforce, put the loop over the button to make sure it slides easily. Add beads if necessary. Reinforce. FIG. 9 shows the completed loop closure.

**10** For a ribbon strap that ties instead of having a button-and-loop closure, follow Steps 1 through 5. Tie the ribbon at the back of the wearer's neck instead of having a closure. This is a very comfortable closure and also allows you to adjust the length.

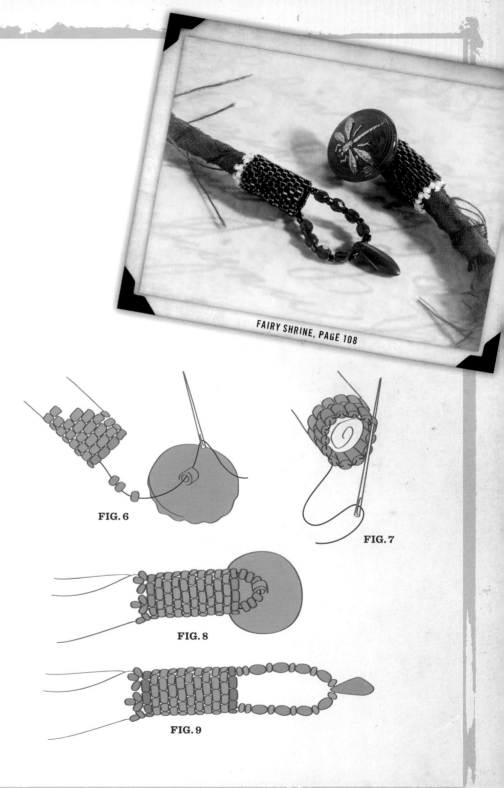

FAIRY SHRINE, PAGE 108

FIG. 6

FIG. 7

FIG. 8

FIG. 9

# Projects

**NOW THAT YOU'VE RAIDED** your jewelry box, gone through your bead stash, and scoured a few flea markets and yard sales, it's time to start creating with all your seemingly disparate objects. Following are some of my favorite projects. Maybe you've gathered materials with a particular project in mind, but if not, let the project that most excites you be a guide. You might even personalize your creation by combining elements—perhaps the beaded chandelier pendant of *Sunset Boulevard,* page 70, with the multi-fiber beaded-bead strap of *Witch's Enchantment,* page 128. Don't be afraid to use objects with sentimental value that you've been saving for a special creation; they'll bring meaning and soul to your projects. It's my sincere hope that you enjoy making these adornments as much as I've enjoyed creating them, so dust off those forgotten things and make something truly magical.

*Washed Ashore, page 100*

## Tales FROM THE Attic

**FINISHED LENGTH:**
Strap, 20" (51 cm)
Pendant, 5¾" (14.5 cm)

A thorough dig through your jewelry box or stash can be as much fun as an exploration in an artifact-filled attic. *Tales from the Attic* uses a variety of materials and beads. Peyote stitch and right-angle weave add color and detail, dressing up the focal crystal and lending an old-world appeal. As you create, imagine the person whose attic might have yielded these seemingly disparate objects.

## MATERIALS

- ☐ 3 × ⅝" (7.6 × 1.5cm) pointed crystal pendant (drop) from a chandelier
- ☐ ¼" (6 mm) Terrifically Tacky double-sided tape
- ☐ 5 g size 11° cylinder beads
- ☐ 3 or 4 fire-polished beads, 3mm, for the crystal
- ☐ 1 fire-polished bead, 4mm crystal, or top-drilled drop to hang from the crystal
- ☐ 2 photos or images to enclose in glass or slides
- ☐ 2 squares or rectangles of beveled glass or microscope slides to fit your picture
- ☐ ¾" (2 cm) copper foil (if using beveled glass) or ¼" (6 mm) copper foil (if using slides), to cover perimeter of glass
- ☐ 3 g size 11° Japanese seed beads
- ☐ 26 fire-polished beads, 3mm, to embellish the top of the right-angle weave

- ☐ 3 g size 11° cylinder beads to match or contrast with the size 11° seed beads
- ☐ 1 vintage watch, empty or intact
- ☐ 1 keyhole finding, 1 × ½" (2.5 × 1.3cm)
- ☐ 8" (20.5 cm) of ⅞" (2.2 cm) wide velvet, satin, grosgrain, or other ribbon
- ☐ 13 jump rings in a variety of sizes
- ☐ 4 or 5 beads, 12mm
- ☐ 1 irregularly shaped bead, about 20mm
- ☐ 36" (91.5 cm) of brass 24-gauge wire
- ☐ 1 toggle clasp, 12mm, or a hook-and-ring closure
- ☐ Beading thread of choice
- ☐ *Optional:* Small tintype image or photo glued to heavy cardstock (if using empty watch)
- ☐ *Optional:* E6000 adhesive (if using empty watch)
- ☐ *Optional:* Beeswax to condition thread

## TOOLS

- ☐ Size 12 beading needle
- ☐ Flush wire cutters
- ☐ Burnishing tool or bone folder
- ☐ Toothpicks
- ☐ Small sharp scissors
- ☐ Round-nose pliers
- ☐ Flat-nose pliers

# TECHNIQUES

- Odd-count flat peyote stitch (20)
- Picot edge for peyote stitch (23)
- Even-count tubular peyote stitch (25)
- Increase in tubular peyote stitch (26)
- Right-angle weave and embellishment (30)
- Join peyote stitch to right-angle weave (32)
- Ladder stitch (34)
- Basic wire wrap (40)
- Foiling (42)
- Picot edge for embroidery (51)
- Ribbon link (52)

BEADED CRYSTAL, VARIATION (PAGE 94)

## STEPS

**1** Place a piece of double-sided tape around the large crystal chandelier drop, just above the widest part of the crystal. Cut and condition a comfortable length of thread and thread the size 12 needle. String an even number of cylinder beads and tie them around the crystal at the top edge of the tape. Leave an 8" (20.5 cm) tail. Stitch several rows of even-count tubular peyote stitch {**FIG. 1**}.

**2** As you work in peyote stitch, you will need to increase as the space becomes too large for 1 bead. Cover the double-sided tape with peyote stitch. Make peaks at the top and bottom by putting on a bead at every other stitch {**FIG. 2**}.

**3** From one of the peaks, start the strand that holds the drop at the bottom tip of the crystal using cylinder beads. A 3mm fire-polished bead looks nice coming from the peak and a 4mm crystal ends the strand below the crystal tip. Use beads with large holes since you will go through them several times to reinforce your work {**FIG. 3**}

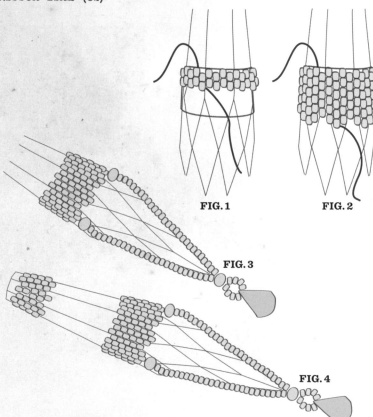

FIG. 1

FIG. 2

FIG. 3

FIG. 4

**4** In **FIG. 4**, the beading on the crystal is complete, but another band of peyote stitch can be added to the top (see variation on page 63).

**5** Pick out an assortment of beads and photos and choose a watch case and keyhole finding. Cut microscope slides to size to fit photos or collage elements. Clean the slides or the beveled glass and place the photos inside.

**6** Foil around the entire edge of the sandwiched glass and photos as described on page 42, overlapping the foil.

**7** Tape along the outside edge of the sandwiched glass and photos with double-sided tape. Leave the plastic coating on. Using size 11° Japanese seed beads, weave a strip of right-angle weave just long enough to fit around the edges of the sandwiched glass. Pull plastic off the tape to expose the adhesive and carefully center the strip of right-angle weave along the center of the tape. Join the ends together with a stitch.

**8** Embellish the top of the right-angle-weave stitches using size 11° seed beads and 3mm crystals {**FIG. 5**}.

**9** Change to peyote stitch, inserting the needle through the 2 beads along the edge and putting 1 size 11° seed bead in between. Continue in peyote stitch. Depending on the thickness of the glass, you may continue to use size 11° seed bead if the glass is thick and not going over the edge of the taped glass sandwich yet. If the glass piece is thin and the next row will start to close over the edge, change to cylinder beads. Skip over the corners, not putting a bead in, stitching from one set of cylinder beads to the other. After the row of cylinder beads, switch to size 15° Japanese seed beads using 1 bead per stitch. Stitch another row of size 15° beads at 2 beads per stitch. Stitch 3 beads in the corners where you have sewn the cylinder beads to each other. Repeat on the other side. On a thicker piece, you may have a different beading sequence on each side.

**10** Make a ladder-stitch loop using size 11° seed beads at each end of the piece. I have 9 ladder stitches using 2 beads per stitch making up the loop.

**11** Carefully place E6000 adhesive along the bottom edge of an empty watch case using a toothpick. Adhere a small tintype or other image, pressing gently. Remove or smooth glue along the outside edge with a toothpick. Set aside to dry completely.

**12** After adhesive has dried, cut the tintype to the edge of the watch case using a pair of small sharp scissors.

**13** Attach a large jump ring to the keyhole and then attach 2 smaller jump rings to that. Using jump rings, attach the watch case to the keyhole and the beaded glass link that you made earlier to the case.

GLASS AND PHOTO COMPONENT

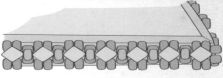

**FIG. 5**

**FIG. 6**

**BEADED CRYSTAL**

**14** Wire-wrap a variety of beads to make a strand 4" to 6" (10 to 15 cm) long. Attach to the keyhole with a jump ring.

**15** Slip two 5.25mm jump rings at the top of the ladder-stitch link and then close a 15mm jump ring through that.

**16** Cut a ribbon about 10" (25.5 cm) long and slip it through the 15mm jump ring. Stitch the ends of the ribbon with a few stitches.

**17** Using cylinder beads, size 15° seed beads, one 3.4mm Japanese drop, and the ribbon, make a Ribbon Link {**FIG. 6**}.

**18** Make a loop of 7 to 9 cylinder beads at the top and tie off the thread. Attach one side of the clasp to the loop with a jump ring.

**19** Slip one, two, or three lengths of chain on a jump ring and close this to the top loop of the wire-wrapped strand. Measure the chains against the other strap and then cut the chain(s) to the desired length. Attach another jump ring and close this to the other side of the clasp.

**20** Put a large jump ring at the bottom of the keyhole, slipping on the crystal before you close it.

### TALES FROM THE ATTIC VARIATION

A toggle clasp, chunky bead, and silk ribbon bound with peyote-stitch tubes give this variation a bold look.

# The Story Pendant

**FINISHED LENGTH:**
42" (106.5 cm)

I wanted to use fabric in a piece, so I rifled through my bead cabinet for something to cover with silk douppioni fabric. A large stone donut caught my eye, and I held the fabric over it. I dug out some large galvanized washers left over from a previous project and added a tintype, a Paris charm, an old key, a locket, and an earring part, setting the stage for what I call *The Story Pendant*. Let the pieces you choose tell a story, real or imagined.

## MATERIALS

- ☐ 1½" (3.8 cm) galvanized washer
- ☐ Tintype image or button to match the size of the washer
- ☐ Charm, button, or cabochon to fit in the center of the washer
- ☐ Double-sided carpet tape
- ☐ Silk fabric slightly larger than the washer
- ☐ ¼" (6 mm) Terrifically Tacky double-sided tape
- ☐ E6000 adhesive
- ☐ 72" (183 cm) of 24-gauge wire (enough to go around the washer, for strap and for dangles)
- ☐ 5 g size 11° Japanese seed beads
- ☐ 50 fire-polished beads or bicone crystals, 3mm
- ☐ 3 g cylinder beads
- ☐ 2 g size 15° Japanese seed beads
- ☐ Assortment of coin pearls, beads, spacers, and crystals
- ☐ 3 round sections from toggle clasps or large jump rings
- ☐ 36" (91.5 cm) silk crinkle ribbon for the top part of the strap
- ☐ 7" (18 cm) of chain to attach to dangles
- ☐ Jump rings in various sizes
- ☐ 1 small bottle and glitter, jewels, beads, or sand to fill it
- ☐ Beading thread
- ☐ *Optional:* Skeleton key; octagonal chandelier part, about 20mm; large drop, 8×40mm
- ☐ *Optional:* Beeswax to condition thread

## TOOLS

- ☐ Size 12 beading needle
- ☐ Small sharp scissors
- ☐ Flush cutters
- ☐ File
- ☐ Round-nose pliers
- ☐ Flat-nose pliers
- ☐ Chain-nose pliers
- ☐ Wire cutters

## TECHNIQUES

> Odd-count flat peyote stitch (20)
> Picot edge on peyote stitch (23)
> Zippering flat peyote stitch into a tube (24)
> Right-angle weave and embellishment (30)
> Join peyote stitch to right-angle weave (32)
> Basic wire wrap (40)

CENTER CHARM DETAIL

## STEPS

**1** Select components to fit inside and on the back of the washer. Cut a tintype image to the same circumference as the washer or use a button that is the same size as the washer (if you prefer, you can resin an image using the doming technique). Choose a charm that will fit inside the washer or on top of the fabric side.

**2** Cover both sides of the washer with double-sided carpet tape and trim to fit {**FIG. 1**}.

**3** Cut a circle of silk larger than the washer. Peel the protective layer of the carpet tape from one side of the washer to expose the adhesive and place the silk over it. Smooth the silk as you adhere it. With a small sharp pair of scissors, cut V shapes in the outer edge of the silk and slits in the inner circle as shown in **FIG. 2**.

**4** Pull the protective layer from the tape on the remaining side of the washer and smooth down the fabric over the washer.

**5** Push the points of silk through the center hole and press it to the underside, making it adhere well.

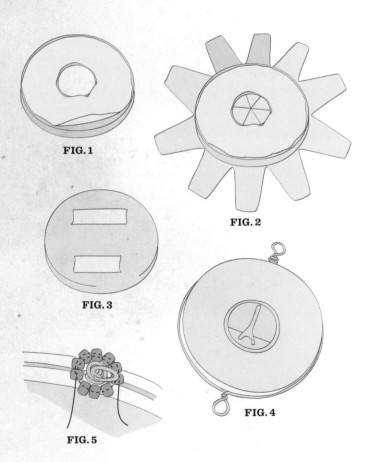

FIG. 1

FIG. 2

FIG. 3

FIG. 4

FIG. 5

**6** Put two strips of double-sided tape on the wrong side of the photo or button that matches the washer size, one near the top and one near the bottom {FIG. 3}.

**7** Place the photo on the back of the washer, lining up the edge and pressing it down. If the front of the washer and the photo have a direction (top and bottom), be sure to place the photo properly so your photo will be centered.

**8** If the charm you've chosen for the center of the washer has loops, cut them off, file the ends down, and glue the charm in the center of the washer on the fabric-covered side with E6000 adhesive.

**9** Cut a piece of 24-gauge wire about 8" (20.5 cm) long. Put double-sided tape around the circumference of the washer. Make a wire wrap in the center of the wire. Place the wire wrap at the bottom of the washer and form the wire around the washer, pressing it firmly onto the tape.

**10** Because the wire wrap is in the center of the wire, there will be two wire tails at the top of the washer. Make the loop to start a wire wrap at the top of the washer with one of the wire tails. Then wrap the loop with both wires to finish. **FIG. 4** shows the wraps at top and bottom of the pendant.

**11** Place a piece of Terrifically Tacky tape along each side of the washer, going from wrap to wrap. Peel off plastic pieces to expose adhesive. Cut and condition a comfortable length of thread and thread a beading needle. With size 11° Japanese seed beads, make the first right-angle-weave stitch around the top wire wrap. You may need up to 10 beads to go around the wrap {FIG. 5}.

**12** Continue the right-angle weave along the edge of the washer to the bottom wire wrap. You may need to adjust the number of beads in the final unit to make a snug fit. {FIG. 6}.

**13** Using size 11° Japanese seed beads and 3mm fire-polished beads or bicone crystals, embellish the right-angle weave as described on page 29.

**14** Close the edge of the beadwork around both sides as follows: with size 11° Japanese seed beads, change from right-angle weave to peyote stitch by inserting the needle through 2 beads at the edge, putting 1 bead on the needle, and passing the needle through the next 2 beads. Repeat all the way around {FIG. 7}.

**15** Change to cylinder beads and continue in peyote stitch. You will put on 2 beads per stitch, inserting the needle into the single bead from the last row {FIG. 8}. If the charm you have chosen for the back of the pendant is thick, then you may need additional rows of size 11° Japanese seed beads before you switch to cylinder beads.

**16** Switch to size 15° seed beads and bring the needle through the cylinder beads, putting 1 size 15° bead between each set. This should cover the edge of the pendant. **FIG. 9** shows a detail of the pendant border.

**17** Repeat on the other side, closing the beadwork over the edge of the pendant.

**18** Begin to make the strap for the pendant. Wire-wrap and connect the coin pearls,

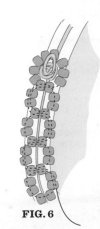

FIG. 6

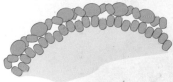

FIG. 7

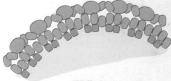

FIG. 8

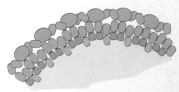

FIG. 9

crystals, and spacers to make two lengths of beaded chain for the strap, each about 4" to 4½" (10 to 11.5 cm) long, attaching the first wire wrap of each section to the top of the pendant. Attach the last wire wrap of each section to the round part of a toggle clasp.

**19** Make two pieces of peyote stitch, each 11 beads wide and 20 rows long (there should be 10 beads up the side when you count). Make a picot edge along each smooth side {FIG. 10}.

**20** Cut the silk crinkle ribbon in half. Pull the cut end of a ribbon through the toggle and fold about ½" (1.3 cm) over. Place one of the peyote pieces you made in Step 19 around the folded ribbon and zipper it closed. To secure the ribbon inside, insert the needle through the tube, go through a bead and bring the needle back through the tube {FIG. 11}.

Do this all the way up the tube. Be sure that you don't pull the thread too tightly when you sew through the tube. Repeat with the other half of the ribbon.

**21** Put the glitter, sand, or other material inside the small bottle. You can use a cork to seal the bottle if your bottle doesn't have a cap or closure. Bead the top of the bottle using tubular peyote stitch and decrease until you close the beadwork over the top of the cap. Make wire wraps on large drops or beads to use as dangles. With jump rings and chain, attach the dangles to the round part of a toggle clasp. On my necklace, I also added a skeleton key and octagonal chandelier part.

**22** Attach the toggle holding the dangles to the bottom of the pendant using 1 or 2 jump rings to complete the pendant.

REVERSE OF CHARM; DANGLES

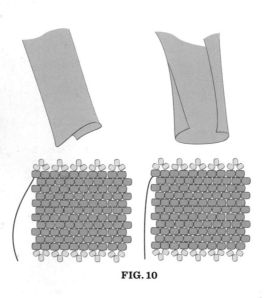

FIG. 10

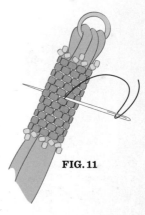

FIG. 11

**THE STORY PENDANT VARIATION**

The Eiffel Tower reappears in a
gold, ruby, and taupe colorway.

# Sunset Boulevard

**FINISHED LENGTH:**
18" (45.5 cm)

Old Hollywood: Crumbling mansions with worn carpets and dusty chandeliers. Norma Desmond slinks dramatically down the curving stairs, past the glittering crystal chandelier, playing her best role yet—she thinks. The old chandelier parts that I find at flea markets and antiques shops always remind me of old movies and the glamour that went with them. Today, you can find pretty much anything on Sunset Boulevard, but when you look past the tourist stops, the tattoo parlors, and the bars, Old Hollywood is still there, chandeliers and all.

## MATERIALS

- ☐ Chandelier crystal drop with hole, about 1⅝" × 2¼" (4 × 5.5cm)
- ☐ Fabric scrap large enough to cover back of chandelier drop
- ☐ Diamond Glaze adhesive
- ☐ ¼" (6 mm) Terrifically Tacky double-sided tape
- ☐ 5 g size 11° Japanese seed beads
- ☐ 40 fire-polished or bicone crystal beads, 3mm
- ☐ 4 g cylinder beads
- ☐ 2 g size 15° Japanese seed beads
- ☐ 24" (61 cm) of 24-gauge wire

- ☐ Assortment of stone, crystal, and pressed-glass beads
- ☐ 16 bead caps and spacers, 5mm to 8mm
- ☐ 16 jump rings, 5.25mm
- ☐ 2 jump rings, 12mm, for ends of wire-wrapped strands
- ☐ 39" (99 cm) of ½" (1.2 cm) wide lightweight ribbon
- ☐ Button with shank, ¾" (2 cm) diameter
- ☐ 8 fire-polished beads, 3mm
- ☐ Dagger bead for closure, 10mm
- ☐ Beading thread of choice
- ☐ *Optional:* Beeswax to condition thread

## TOOLS

- ☐ Small paintbrush
- ☐ Size 12 beading needle
- ☐ Flush cutters
- ☐ Round-nose pliers
- ☐ Flat-nose pliers
- ☐ Chain-nose pliers

## TECHNIQUES

- Odd-count flat peyote stitch (20)
- Right-angle weave and embellishment (30)
- Join peyote stitch to right-angle weave (32)
- Basic wire wrap (40)
- Ribbon strap clasp (54)

EMBELLISHED EDGE

**FIG. 1**

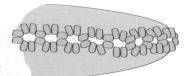

**FIG. 2**

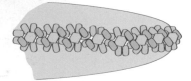

**FIG. 3**

## STEPS

**1** Clean the large chandelier drop. Cut a piece of fabric larger than the drop. Pour a small amount of Diamond Glaze adhesive into a paper cup or small foil pan.

**2** With a small paintbrush, brush the back of the chandelier pendant with Diamond Glaze and adhere the fabric smoothly.

**3** Brush a generous coating of Diamond Glaze on the back of the fabric applied in the previous step. Set aside and let dry.

**4** Trim the fabric to the edge of the drop.

**5** Apply double-sided tape around the perimeter of the drop {**FIG. 1**}. You may need to trim the tape if the edge of your drop is narrow.

**6** Cut and condition a comfortable length of thread. Thread a needle on one end of the thread. With size 11° Japanese seed beads, make a strip of right-angle weave with 8 beads per stitch, all the way around the perimeter of the drop, joining the first and last stitch {**FIG. 2**}.

**7** With size 11° Japanese seed beads and 3mm fire-polished beads or bicone crystals, embellish the stitches all the way around the crystal {**FIG. 3**}.

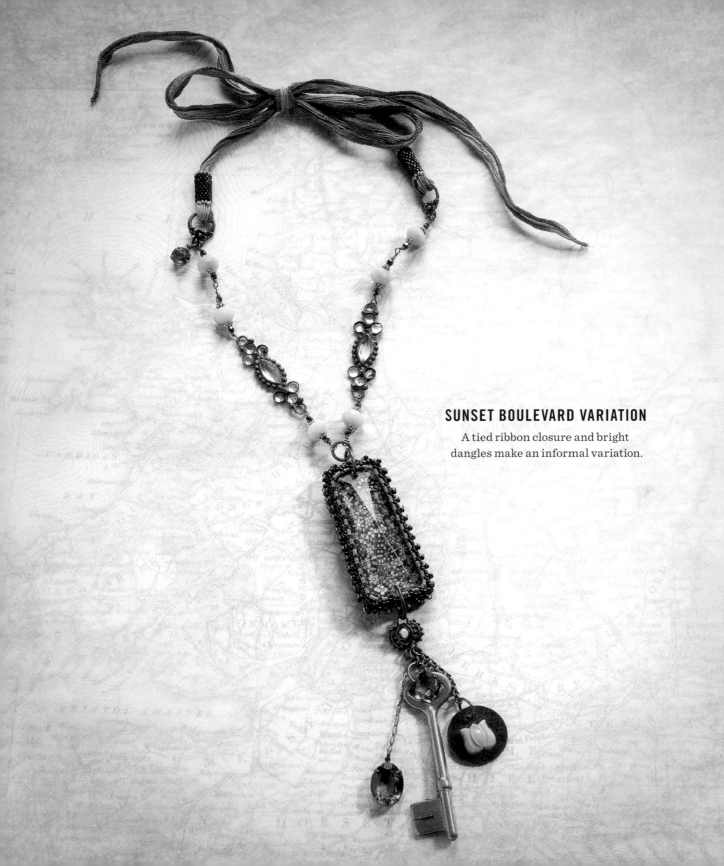

**SUNSET BOULEVARD VARIATION**

A tied ribbon closure and bright
dangles make an informal variation.

**8** Change to peyote stitch. The needle should be exiting from a set of 2 beads along the front of the crystal (you'll do the back later). Put 1 size 11° bead on the needle and pass the needle through the next set of 2 beads. Continue around the drop.

**9** Depending on the thickness of your crystal, you may use size 11° beads in this row or switch to cylinder beads. Continue in peyote stitch by putting 2 beads on the needle and passing the needle through 1 bead from the last row all the way around, using 2 beads per stitch {FIG. 4}.

**10** Switching to size 15° Japanese seed beads, continue in peyote stitch, using 1 bead per stitch and passing the needle through sets of 2 cylinder beads, around the drop {FIG. 5}. Repeat Steps 8 to 10 on the other side of the crystal.

**11** With about 10" (25.5 cm) of wire, make a wire wrap at the center of the wire through the hole in the top of the crystal. Use both ends of the wire together when making the wrap and don't worry if it's not perfect—you'll add embellishment later {FIG. 6}.

**12** Make two strands, each about 4" (10 cm) long, of wire-wrapped beads by wire-wrapping each bead and joining the individual wraps with jump rings {FIG. 7}.

**13** Join the bottom ends of both strands to the wire wrap at the top of the chandelier crystal, using 2 jump rings per end.

**14** Use cylinder beads to make four rectangles of peyote stitch, each 9 beads wide and 18 rows long (count 9 beads down the side). Make a picot edge on only one side of each piece.

**15** Cut two 16" (40.6 cm) pieces and fold each piece into fourths. Use these folded pieces of ribbon, the four peyote rectangles created in Step 14, the button, 3mm fire-polished beads, dagger bead, and cylinder beads to complete Steps 3 through 9 of the Ribbon Strap Clasp (page 54).

**16** Cut a length of ribbon about 7" (18 cm). Wrap the ribbon around the wire wrap at the top of the crystal. Tie once in back, bring to the front, and tie again. Pull tight to secure or make a few stitches with needle and thread to complete the project.

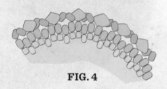

FIG. 4

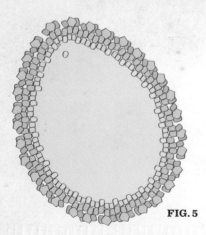

FIG. 5

FIG. 6

FIG. 7

# Telling a Story

## How to Use Your Unearthed Treasures

There are several ways to approach creating jewelry. The first is as simple as picking out a project from this book, gathering the necessary materials, and beginning to create. I'd like to suggest some alternative methods as well.

➤ Look through the objects you have collected. Does one stand out? Does it vibrate in your hands? If you have an object that you have been saving, just waiting for the right project, ask yourself which project might make the best use of it. Do you want it to be the focus of the piece or do you want it to complement other elements?

➤ If there's a project that excites you and you know that is the piece you want to make, gather what you need to get started. As you progress, choose the objects to embellish, letting the story unfold as you go along. I seldom gather every material needed at the beginning, preferring to put together just the basics. As I need more materials, I look through my bead or mixed-media stash. Sometimes a bead or object will come to mind as I'm working, and I'll stop to find it. This is my preferred way to work. All of the materials you'll need for a project are listed at the beginning of the instructions in order of use. Make a mental note of what you might like to use or get it out and put it in a nice dish on your work area so you can glance at it as you create. It might still be the item to use when you arrive at that section of the pattern, or you may decide on something else. Allow yourself the flexibility of changing your mind about the components as you work on the projects.

➤ This method is a bit like a game: close your eyes and move your hand over your drawer or box of found objects. Choose one randomly and pick the project that you believe it's most suited for. You might even feel a tingle in the palm of your hand as you do this. I like to hold an object in my hand, close my eyes, and see if any images come to mind, especially if it is something that has had a previous owner. This technique is known as psychometry, a psychic technique of divining history or mental pictures from an object. An antiques shop is a very good place to experiment or practice. I don't consider myself to be a psychic, but I do sometimes see images or get a certain feeling from holding items.

➤ Another way to get started is to list all of the projects and the components on a sheet of paper. Use calligraphy or a computer font that pleases you. Cut the paper into strips with the names on them and put the strips into a jar. They don't have to be folded, but you can slightly curl them if you like. When you're feeling stuck, reach in the jar, pull out a slip, and start creating. If you don't have all the materials for the project, look at what you do have and see if you can substitute and perhaps create something you like even better than the original idea. Pull out another strip and figure out a way to combine the projects.

➤ If all that sounds just a bit too hokey, do what I often do: pick out the objects or projects that are the most visually pleasing to you. There are times when you want to put spirit into your work and other times when you just want to make something pretty. Both are valid and both approaches contain the energy you used to create it: what you were thinking, what you were feeling, and therefore your essence.

# Memory Keeper

**FINISHED LENGTH:**
43" (109 cm)

There's something deeply satisfying about making a piece of beaded jewelry that holds surprises, and that is what *Memory Keeper* is all about. Named for its large locket, you can remove the pendant and wear this as a simple multi-strand necklace. If you prefer a regular clasp to the ribbon ties, that's easy to do, although the ties allow for length adjustment. To begin *Memory Keeper,* think of the mood or memory you are conjuring up. What colors best express that mood? What can you put in the locket to evoke a memory? Let the piece evolve as you work.

## MATERIALS

*For the multi-strand necklace:*

- ☐ 2 metal or plastic thimbles with a hole drilled in the top center of each
- ☐ 10 g cylinder beads in one or more colors
- ☐ 15 g size 11° Japanese seed beads in main color
- ☐ 660 fire-polished beads or bicone crystals, 3mm, or size 8° seed beads (or a combination)
- ☐ Jeweler's glue
- ☐ 12" (30.5 cm) of 24-gauge wire
- ☐ 36" (91.5 cm) silk crinkle ribbon
- ☐ 5 g size 15° seed beads in one or more colors

*For the pendant:*

- ☐ 1 locket or pendant
- ☐ Velvet fabric, polymer clay face cabochon, stone cabochon, photograph, or other ephemera to decorate inside of locket
- ☐ E6000 adhesive
- ☐ 3 g cylinder beads in two or more colors
- ☐ 3 g size 15° seed beads
- ☐ 3 snaps, size 3/0
- ☐ 1 jump ring, 5.25mm, to attach locket
- ☐ Beading thread of choice
- ☐ *Optional:* Stone drop, about 30mm, and 24-gauge wire to attach it
- ☐ *Optional:* Beeswax to condition thread

## TOOLS

- ☐ Fine-point permanent marker
- ☐ Size 12 beading needle
- ☐ Round-nose pliers
- ☐ Flat-nose pliers

# TECHNIQUES

- Odd-count flat peyote stitch (20)
- Picot edge for peyote stitch (23)
- Zippering flat peyote stitch into a tube (24)
- Even-count tubular peyote stitch (25)
- Decrease in tubular peyote stitch (28)
- Stitch in the ditch (29)
- Right-angle weave and embellishment (30)
- Cranky wrap (41)
- Sewing snaps to beadwork (44)
- Beaded thimble (46)
- Beaded cabochon (48)

LOCKET, OPEN VIEW

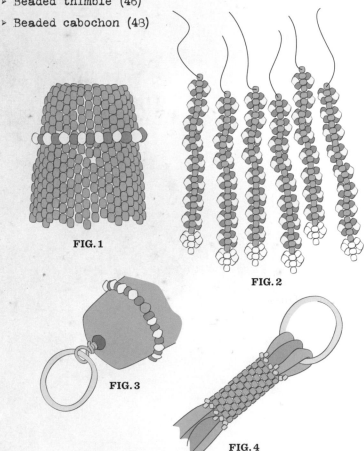

FIG. 1

FIG. 2

FIG. 3

FIG. 4

## STEPS

**1** Using a fine-point permanent marker, color the bottom edge of both thimbles. The marker may show; if you are using a colored plastic thimble, color it black or brown if the original color doesn't match the beads you're using. Using cylinder beads and even-count tubular peyote stitch, bead the thimbles and set aside {FIG. 1}. You should be left with a circle of beads at the top of the thimble after you finish covering it with the cylinder beads.

**2** Using size 11° Japanese seed beads, begin right-angle-weave strands to go inside the thimble caps. The first circle of right-angle weave will contain 8 beads. Because the following stitches will share 2 beads of the previous stitch, you will put on 6 beads. Be sure to leave an 8" (20.5 cm) tail. When the strand reaches the length you desire (55 or more stitches), embellish on both sides with 3mm fire-polished beads, 3mm crystals, size 8° seed beads, or any combination of these. Complete all the necessary strands; my thimble caps held 6 strands {FIG. 2}. You should have an 8" (20.5 cm) tail on each end; if your working thread is longer, trim it to 8" (20.5 cm).

**3** Gather all the threads at the end of the strands, twist them together, and tie into a knot as close to the beadwork as possible. Do this at both ends. With jewelry glue, glue the knot well. I also put some glue on the threads above the knot. Set aside. When the glue is completely dry, trim the threads about ⅛" (2 mm) above the knot.

**4** With a 2½" (6.5 cm) piece of 24-gauge wire, make a bend 1¼" (3.2 cm) from one end. Loop the wire under the knot you made in Step 3 and make a basic wire wrap on top. Repeat at other end. Slip on the beaded thimble cap and one 3mm fire-polished bead and make a wire wrap on top of the thimble. Do this at both ends. The 3mm fire-polish beaded should sit down inside the circle of beads mentioned in Step 1 and will cover any part of the thimble still visible {FIG. 3}. If you are using the round part of a toggle clasp instead of jump rings, make the top wrap with the clasp inside the wrap.

**5** To make the strap, begin by cutting a length of crinkle ribbon in half and set aside.

**6** Make two pieces of odd-count flat peyote stitch, each 11 beads wide and long enough to wrap over the ribbon when it has been doubled. Make a picot edge on each smooth side. Thread the ribbon through one of the jump rings or toggles and slide up so that the peyote stitch piece will cover it. Wrap the peyote stitch piece around the ribbon, zipper closed, and sew through the tube and down the length of it to secure the ribbon inside {FIG. 4}. Repeat on the other side.

**7** Glue the ephemera you've chosen inside the locket. If you wish to do beading for the locket, complete that and glue in place. If you've chosen a collage piece, prepare all the pieces and then glue them inside with E6000 adhesive. Set aside to dry.

**8** Make a piece of odd-count peyote stitch that is 21 beads wide and long enough to wrap around the strands plus at least ½" (1.3 cm) overlap for snaps. Make peaks on one end and decrease the other end to a point. Make a picot edge on both long edges using size 15° Japanese seed beads {FIG. 5}.

**9** Wrap the piece around the beaded multi-strands and mark where you will be sewing on the snaps. Sew 1 snap at the center of the point and the other 2 at the spots before the decreases begin {FIG. 6}. Sew on both the male and female parts of the snaps, checking that you have placed them on the correct side of the beadwork.

PENDANT AND STRIP WITH SNAPS

FIG. 5

FIG. 6

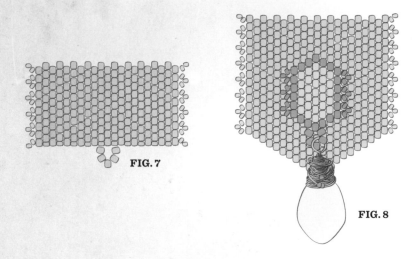

FIG. 7

FIG. 8

**10** Close the piece around the multi-strands so you can find the row that will be at the bottom; this is where you will make a loop of beads to slip the jump ring through. Take the piece off so you can bead the loop. Make a loop of 5 cylinder beads {**FIG. 7**}. Reinforce well.

**11** Make a small flap to hang the stone drop. Using the cranky-wrap method described on page 41, wire-wrap a large flat stone drop. Set aside.

**12** Slip the woven piece you made in Step 8 back on the multi-strands to locate the top, then remove it. With cylinder beads, stitch in the ditch near the top of the piece. This flap is 7 beads wide, so you will stitch in the ditch 4 beads, making sure that you loop under the thread on the fourth bead and then go back through the bead. When you have 6 beads stacked on top of each other at the side of the flap, decrease to a point. Make a picot edge using size 15° Japanese seed beads up one side. Make the other end into a point and make a picot edge using size 15° Japanese seed beads on the other side.

**13** Make a loop of 5 cylinder beads and slip on the wire-wrapped stone drop before attaching the loop and reinforcing {**FIG. 8**}.

**14** Decorate the front of the locket with beadwork or a piece of filigree if desired.

**15** Close the pendant piece around the multi-strand necklace to complete the project.

MULTI-STRAND NECKLACE WITH BEADED-THIMBLE CAPS

# Setting Up a Creative Space

Take a look around your work space. So often we are mean-minded to ourselves when we sit down to create. We chain ourselves to our desk with such single-mindedness that any desire or passion quickly turns to fear, and creativity flies out the window on black crow's wings.

How do you feel about the space where you create? Is your desk or table pleasing to you? Can you see out a window? If not, do you have pictures that inspire you and that you find beautiful? Do you have nice dishes or trays to put things in? Is your space functional? This may sound silly, but give your space some thought, especially if you feel stuck. We deny ourselves beauty, yet we expect to create it. When an area is void of life, it will be void of creativity.

These questions come out of my own experience. I have been stuck, and I have sat at a table I thought was ugly in a room that didn't inspire me and wondered why I didn't feel like creating anything.

Today, the space where I create could not be considered beautiful by any stretch of the imagination, but I sit at a desk I love. It is small; the top is marred and the varnish is coming off in places. I like its weathered beauty. The desk is positioned in front of a window, something that's very important to me. There are pretty trays, one for beading and one for holding various projects I am working on. There are pretty dishes for beads. A cigar box holds my beading tools. The unit where I store my beads was my biggest purchase and worth every penny. I have a few pictures that I love hanging on the walls. There's a lot of shelving in this room, lined with box after box of supplies. I like to do a lot of different things, and this room reflects that. The materials I love surround and inspire me to start on something right now.

These things were not expensive; they were purchased over time as I discovered how I wanted to store my supplies and what was most practical. For me, functionality and ease of working are most important, and I fit beauty in where I can.

Your space should be a place you enjoy being in just as mine is, a place that inspires you to create. Your supplies should be easy to get to so that you aren't constantly hunting for things. Make your space functional and add beautiful elements as you go along.

# Dream Vessel

**FINISHED LENGTH:**
36" (91.5 cm)

One of my early forays in combining beads with other materials was a series of polymer clay vessels covered in beadwork called *The Sacrifice Series*. When I was gathering my thoughts on this book, I thought of that series. The original vessels were completely covered or layered with beadwork, but I decided to design a project that would go faster yet still provide interesting surface texture. I love the idea of wearing a small container that opens, holding a scrap of a poem or a tiny sketch.

## MATERIALS

- ☐ 1 package polymer clay
- ☐ Small quartz crystal point
- ☐ Basket-style bead cap (mine is from Aria Design Studios)
- ☐ 4" × 4" (10 × 10 cm) scrap of lace
- ☐ White glue
- ☐ 10 g size 11° seed beads in two or more colors
- ☐ 20 to 30 round crystals, 2mm, in one to three colors
- ☐ 12" (30.5 cm) of 24- or 22-gauge wire

- ☐ 2 head pins
- ☐ Jump rings in assorted sizes
- ☐ Assortment of glass beads, crystals, pearls, spacers, and bead caps
- ☐ 36" (91.5 cm) silk crinkle ribbon for the top part of the strap
- ☐ Crystal, 4mm
- ☐ Beading thread of choice
- ☐ *Optional:* Beeswax to condition thread

## TOOLS

- ☐ Pasta machine or rolling pin
- ☐ Cutting tool for clay
- ☐ Sculpting tool for clay
- ☐ Fabric scissors
- ☐ Paintbrush for glue
- ☐ Pen or pencil
- ☐ Glass or cup
- ☐ Size 12 beading needle
- ☐ Flush cutters
- ☐ Round-nose pliers
- ☐ 2 pairs of flat-nose pliers
- ☐ Small sharp scissors

# TECHNIQUES

➤ Right-angle weave and embellishment (30)

➤ Basic wire wrap (40)

➤ Opening and closing a jump ring (41)

**VESSEL CAP**

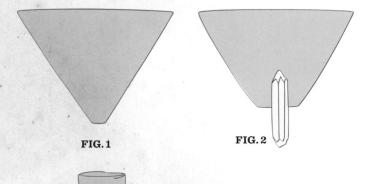

FIG. 1

FIG. 2

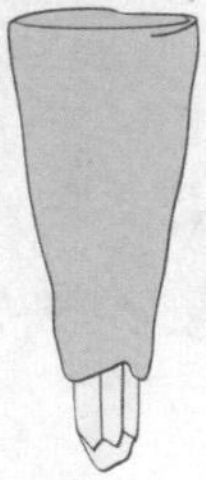

FIG. 3

FIG. 4

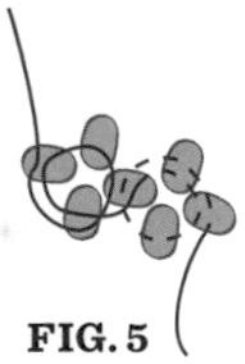

FIG. 5

## STEPS

**1** Begin with the polymer clay vessel. Condition clay and roll out to desired thickness (I used the thickest setting on a pasta machine). Cut the rolled clay into a triangular shape and cut off one of the points of the triangle {**FIG. 1**}. To make the vessel, I used a cutting tool and a sculpting tool made for polymer clay.

**2** Place the crystal at the bottom of the triangle (where you've cut off a point) so it will emerge from the vessel {**FIG. 2**}.

**3** Beginning at the crystal, join the edges of the clay. Press the clay tightly around the crystal. Continue to join the seam of the vessel, pressing the edges together and smoothing with the sculpting tool. Trim the top to make it fairly level {**FIG. 3**}.

**4** This vessel uses a basket- or cage-style bead cap as a cap. Fit the cap on the vessel. If it doesn't fit, stretch the clay gently with your fingers until the cap inserts in the top easily but is snug enough that the clay will hold it {**FIG. 4**}. Shape the vessel a bit, giving it a more organic shape. Bake according to manufacturer's instructions and let cool completely.

**5** Cut a piece of lace that will fit completely around the vessel in its approximate shape. The lace should overlap and extend out from the top and bottom (you'll trim it later). Wrap the lace around the vessel.

**6** Brush a thick coat of white glue on the vessel and press the lace into it. Coat the top of the lace, making sure it adheres to the surface and does not lift up anywhere. Don't fold the edges over the top and do not press the lace against the crystal. If you happen to get glue on your crystal, let it dry and scrape it off with your fingernail. Put a pen or pencil in a glass and place the vessel upside down on it; let dry completely. Trim the excess lace to the top edge and to the crystal at the bottom.

**7** To bead the vessel and cap, begin by cutting and conditioning a comfortable length of thread. Thread a needle on one end of the thread. You will not need a stop bead or a knot.

**8** Do 2 stitches of right-angle weave, 4 beads per circle {**FIG. 5**}.

**9** Lay the beadwork against the vessel. Bring the needle under the lace and then back through the bead {**FIG. 6**}. Make a few more stitches, securing the beadwork to the lace every other stitch. Put a needle on the tail thread, secure it to the lace, and then tie off the thread by weaving through the beadwork, following the existing thread paths.

**10** Continue, letting the beadwork wander down the side, and curving the line {**FIG. 7**}.

**11** When you get to a previous strand, connect it, circle to the other side, and continue {**FIG. 8**}.

**VESSEL WITH BEADWORK**

FIG. 6

FIG. 7

FIG. 8

➤➤ *tips*

If you don't have a dedicated pasta machine for polymer clay, use a rolling pin, but remember that it can no longer be used for food.

I bake my pieces on a thin piece of wood in a large toaster oven. I advise against using a regular oven to bake polymer clay.

Do not pull the thread too tight or pull up when you are sewing through the lace or you may detach it. Be especially careful around the top edge.

Add a bead of another color here and there for contrast.

To tie off thread and begin a new one, weave around, go under a few threads twice, and weave through a few more beads. Clip or burn threads.

To add new thread, pull the thread through a few beads, leaving a 2" (5 cm) tail. Hold the tail down with your thumb. Go under a few threads, weave around until you are where you left off, and clip or burn the tail thread.

**12** When you've completed the beadwork to your satisfaction, add some sparkle by sewing along the edge of the strands, adding a 2mm crystal here and there. You can span a small area by adding a few seed beads with a crystal as well. Tie off thread.

**13** Cut a 3" (7.5 cm) piece of 24- or 22-gauge wire and make a wire wrap at one end.

**14** On a head pin, thread an assortment of beads and bead caps that will dangle inside the vessel. Wire-wrap the top. Open a 4mm jump ring and slide on the wrapped loop made in Step 15 and the dangle made in this step. Close the jump ring {**FIG. 9**}.

**15** Place the wire through the hole in the basket-style cap and place an assortment of beads and spacers on the top. Make a wire-wrapped loop at the top {**FIG. 10**}.

**16** Close a 15mm jump ring through the top wire wrap.

**17** For the strap on this pendant, I attached a crinkle silk cord with a lark's-head knot and a small dangle that I made by wire-wrapping a 4mm bicone crystal and attaching it to the front of the knot with a 6mm jump ring. There is no clasp on this cord—it ties at the back of the neck.

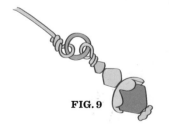

FIG. 9

FIG. 10

**DREAM VESSEL VARIATION**

Black lace and velvet ribbon
make a glamorous necklace.

# *Alter Ego*

**FINISHED LENGTH:**
Strap, 18¼" (46.5 cm)
Pendant, 5¾" (14.5 cm)

I believe that what you don't see when wearing a piece of jewelry is as important as what you do see, so I've often created reversible designs. They're enjoyable to make, add an element of surprise, and make the most of the available design area. For this piece, you'll make the cabochon focal pieces yourself, so the subject matter, color, size, materials, and shape are open to your creativity. Create a Jekyll and Hyde piece, Vintage/Modern, Winter/Spring, or continue a theme on both sides as I did to create a mythic story. My pendant has a photograph on one side and a collage made with butterfly wings and paper text on the other.

## MATERIALS

- Photograph in size desired for pendant
- Heavy paper (Bristol board or cardstock), slightly larger than photograph
- Oval or circle template
- A few lines of text from a book or other collage materials
- Decoupage gel such as Mod Podge
- 5 butterfly or dragonfly wings to resin (or rubber stamp with wing image that will allow you to make your own from plastic or shrink plastic)
- Waxed paper
- Two-part resin
- Beading foundation
- ¼" (6 mm) wide Terrifically Tacky double-sided tape
- 6 g size 15° seed beads in two colors plus two additional colors in small amounts for accents
- 4 g size 11° seed beads in one color
- 1 brass earring filigree for bail
- 1 decorative brass jump ring, 6mm
- 5 locust wings
- Assortment of brass filigree bead caps and jump rings in various sizes

- 5 eyelets, 4mm
- 1 glass bead, 10mm
- 5 bicone crystals, 3mm
- 4" (10 cm) of 24-gauge wire
- Silk fabric or ribbon, 36" × 1¼" (91.5 × 3.2 cm)
- 2.5 g cylinder beads in one color
- 1 shank-style button, ¾" (2 cm) diameter
- 8 fire-polished beads, 3mm
- 1 dagger bead
- 6" (15 cm) narrow silk ribbon ⅛" (3 mm) wide
- 1 glass bead, 6mm to 8mm
- 4 filigree natural brass bead caps
- 1 brass head pin
- Beading thread of choice
- Sewing thread to match silk fabric
- *Optional:* Beeswax to condition thread
- *Optional:* Permanent marker to color beading foundation
- *Optional:* E6000 adhesive

## TOOLS

- Small paintbrush
- Tweezers
- Cotton swabs
- Scissors
- Size 12 beading needle
- Popsicle stick
- Toothpicks or straight pins
- Round-nose pliers
- 2 pairs of flat-nose pliers
- Flush cutters
- Eyelet setter or Crop-a-Dile eyelet setting tool
- Handsewing needle

# TECHNIQUES

- ➤ Basic wire wrap (40)
- ➤ Opening and closing a jump ring (41)
- ➤ Beaded cabochon (48)
- ➤ Ribbon strap clasp (54)

LOCUST-WING DANGLES

## STEPS

*Note: Real butterfly or dragonfly wings are fragile. Use tweezers to pick them up and place them on the decoupage gel and then very lightly press down with a cotton swab, rolling gently to press and burnish the wings in place.*

**1** Begin by making the pendant. With a small paintbrush, coat an old photograph with decoupage gel. If your photo is very thin, adhere it to a piece of heavy paper. Let dry. Press in a book for a few hours.

**2** Cut a piece of heavy paper and lightly draw an oval or other pendant shape so you know where to place the butterfly wings. Coat the shape with decoupage gel and carefully place the butterfly wings on it. Use tweezers to pick up the wings and place them on the decoupage gel and then very lightly press down with a cotton swab, rolling gently to burnish the wings in place. Let dry for a few minutes and apply a coat of decoupage gel. Let dry.

**3** Place the oval template over the piece, mark the oval, and cut out with scissors. Do the same with the photograph. You now have two oval shapes, one a photograph and one a butterfly wing collage.

**4** Cut out words from book text or other collage materials with scissors, paint a bit of decoupage gel on the collage where desired, and use tweezers to apply the cut-out words. Burnish gently with a cotton swab. Apply a coat of decoupage gel over top and let dry completely.

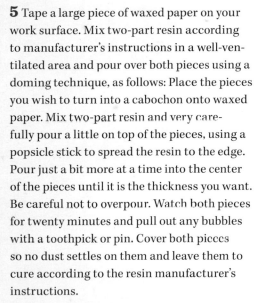

**FIG. 1**

PENDANT, REVERSE SIDE

**5** Tape a large piece of waxed paper on your work surface. Mix two-part resin according to manufacturer's instructions in a well-ventilated area and pour over both pieces using a doming technique, as follows: Place the pieces you wish to turn into a cabochon onto waxed paper. Mix two-part resin and very carefully pour a little on top of the pieces, using a popsicle stick to spread the resin to the edge. Pour just a bit more at a time into the center of the pieces until it is the thickness you want. Be careful not to overpour. Watch both pieces for twenty minutes and pull out any bubbles with a toothpick or pin. Cover both pieces so no dust settles on them and leave them to cure according to the resin manufacturer's instructions.

**6** Adhere the resin "cabochons" you have made to the beading foundation with either E6000 glue or double-sided tape. Cut and condition a comfortable length of beading thread, thread a beading needle, and tie a knot at the end. Do not use a double thread.

**7** Begin with one of the cabochons and size 15° seed beads. Stitch a row of backstitch around the cabochon.

**8** Bring the thread out of one of the beads. Still using size 15° seed beads, put 3 beads on the needle, skip 3 beads, and go through the fourth bead. Change colors if you like or use a different color for the center bead. Adjust the last few stitches if it doesn't work out evenly {**FIG. 1**}. Tie off thread.

**9** Working on the wrong side, trim the excess foundation to the edge of the beadwork.

**10** Repeat on the other cabochon, cutting a longer thread. Do not tie off the thread after stitching.

**11** Apply double-sided tape or E6000 adhesive along the entire surface of the back of one

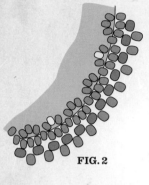

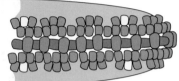

**FIG. 2**

**FIG. 3**

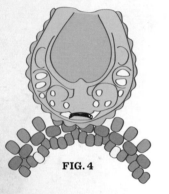

**FIG. 4**

of the cabochons and press the 2 cabochons wrong sides together, pressing firmly all the way around.

**12** With size 11° seed beads, make a picot edge all the way around, sewing through both layers of the foundation {**FIGS. 2 AND 3**}.

**13** Using both round-nose and flat-nose pliers, bend a brass earring filigree to use as a bail. Sew the bail to the top center of the pendant, bringing the thread through both ends to sew the bail securely to the top. Reinforce by going through several times {**FIG. 4**}.

**14** Work the thread to the bottom of the piece and sew a 6mm decorative jump ring to the center bottom. Reinforce well. Make sure you are not sewing the thread across the join in the jump ring. Tie off thread in the beadwork.

**15** To make the locust-wing dangles, tape a sheet of waxed paper on heavy cardboard or a tray. Place several locust wings on the paper. Mix two-part resin. With a small paintbrush, coat one side of the wings with resin. Cover and let cure overnight. Turn the wings over and repeat. Let cure overnight.

**16** Mix resin again. This time, pour the resin very slowly and use a toothpick to pull the resin out toward the edges of the wings (do not allow the resin to run over the edges). Cover and let cure overnight. Turn the wings over, mix resin, and repeat.

**17** With an eyelet setter or Crop-a-Dile tool, set eyelets into the top of the wings.

**18** To make the dangle, bend the largest filigree bead cap so the ends splay out somewhat (you will attach the wings using jump rings).

**CLASP WITH BEADED TUBES**

Make a wire-wrapped link using a variety of filigree bead caps, the 10mm glass bead, and 3 bicone crystals.

**19** Set eyelets into the tops of the locust wings using an eyelet setter.

**20** Attach the wings to the filigree cap using a variety of jump rings. Attach a wing to the bottom of the glass bead {**FIG. 5**}.

**21** Attach the entire dangle to the 6mm brass jump ring at the bottom of the beaded cab with a jump ring.

**22** To make the strap, tear silk fabric along the grain into two strips 18" × 1¼" (45.5 × 3.2 cm) and fold each in half with wrong sides together.

**23** Cut a length of sewing thread 12" (30.5 cm) long, thread a handsewing needle, and tie a knot at the end.

**24** Gather one end of each strip of fabric together and bring the needle through the layers about ¾" (2 cm) from the end and wrap tightly around {**FIG. 6**}. Sew through a few times and tie off the thread. Do not repeat on the other ends yet.

**25** Using the prepared silk strips, cylinder beads, size 15° seed beads, the button, 3mm fire-polished beads, and 1 dagger bead, make a ribbon strap clasp.

**26** Decorate the silk strips to complete the necklace. I have tied some additional thin silk ribbon around the ribbon neckpiece and added a jump ring and a wire-wrapped bead on one side {**FIG. 7**}.

STEP 26 DETAIL

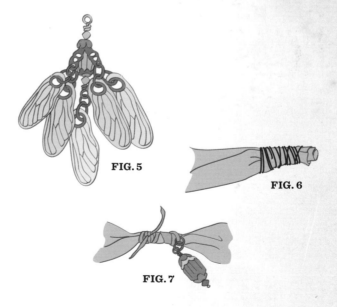

FIG. 5

FIG. 6

FIG. 7

# *Memoir*

**FINISHED LENGTH:**
29" (73.5 cm)

With this bead-covered sketchbook on a bejeweled chain, you'll never be caught without place to record your brilliant artistic ideas. Exchange the long neck strap for a short loop and attach this elegant book to a purse or backpack. Make several and decorate a cigar box to keep them in. Looking back through them will jog your memory of the time and place that you drew an image, wrote a quote, or glued in a ticket stub. If you don't want to make a beaded chain for the strap or hanging loop, try crinkle ribbon, beaded ribbon links, spiral rope, or other woven strap, fibers, or linked jewelry components.

## MATERIALS

- ☐ 1 blank book, 2" × 1¾" (5 × 4.5 cm)
- ☐ Acrylic gesso or acrylic paint
- ☐ 20 g cylinder beads in two or more colors
- ☐ Cabochon, 18x25mm or 25x30mm
- ☐ Beading foundation
- ☐ E6000 adhesive or ½" (1.3 cm) Terrifically Tacky double-sided tape
- ☐ 5 g size 15° seed beads in two or three colors
- ☐ 5 g size 11° seed beads
- ☐ 1 toggle clasp
- ☐ 72" (91.5 cm) of 24-gauge wire
- ☐ 160 assorted beads that vary in color and size
- ☐ 50 jump rings, 5.25mm
- ☐ 1 bar portion of a toggle clasp
- ☐ Beading thread of choice
- ☐ *Optional:* Beeswax to condition thread

## TOOLS

- ☐ Paintbrush
- ☐ Piece of aluminum foil, paper plate, or palette for paint
- ☐ Size 12 beading needle
- ☐ Small sharp scissors
- ☐ Flush cutters
- ☐ Round-nose pliers
- ☐ Two pairs of flat-nose pliers
- ☐ *Optional:* Permanent marker

## TECHNIQUES

- ▷ Odd-count flat peyote stitch (20)
- ▷ Picot edge on peyote stitch (23)
- ▷ Basic wire wrap (40)
- ▷ Opening and closing a jump ring (41)
- ▷ Beaded cabochon (43)

BEADED BOOK

### STEPS

**1** Pour a small amount of acrylic gesso or paint onto a piece of aluminum foil, paper plate, or palette. With a paintbrush, paint the front and back cover of the blank book with acrylic gesso or acrylic paint. Let dry thoroughly. Paint the inside front and back covers. Let dry.

**2** Using cylinder beads, bead a piece of peyote stitch that will cover the entire book from front bottom edge to the back bottom edge and will go to the side edges of the book. Use a pattern you like or make up a random pattern as you go.

**3** Adhere the cabochon on the beading foundation using E6000 adhesive or double-sided tape.

**4** With size 15° seed beads, backstitch around the cabochon.

**5** Continuing with the size 15° seed beads and using the first backstitch row as a base, peyote-stitch a bezel around the cabochon. Make peaks on the last row by skipping every other stitch or put on 3 beads, skip an up-bead, and go through the next up-bead, repeating all the way around to enclose the bezel over the cab.

**6** With size 11° seed beads, do another row of backstitch around the cabochon.

**7** Working on the wrong side, trim the excess foundation with small sharp scissors, being sure not to clip any stitches. Color the edge of the foundation with a permanent marker if desired.

**8** With two colors of size 15° seed beads, make a picot edge all around the cabochon.

**9** Place a piece of double-sided tape or put a spot of glue on the wrong side of the cabochon and adhere it to the beadwork.

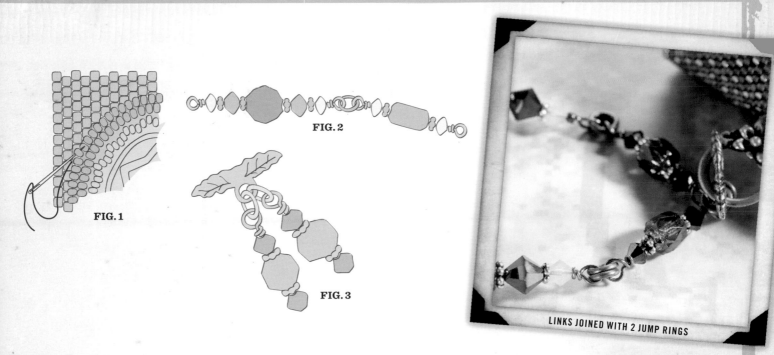

**FIG. 2**

**FIG. 1**

**FIG. 3**

LINKS JOINED WITH 2 JUMP RINGS

**10** With the working thread, sew the cabochon to the beadwork by stitching around the circumference. I keep my stitches between the bezel and the row of size 11° seed beads. **FIG. 1** shows the attached cabochon.

**11** Make a picot edge on each long side of the peyote strip.

**12** Find the top center of the beadwork and sew the round portion of a toggle clasp at that point. Reinforce well.

**13** Cover the front and the back with double-sided tape or glue. Do not put any glue or tape along the spine, or it will not open correctly.

**14** Carefully place the beadwork onto the book, making sure all edges are even. Press the beadwork firmly onto the tape or glue.

**15** For the strap, begin by wire-wrapping 21 links with the assortment of beads. Do not link them together.

**16** Join the links together using one {**FIG. 2**} or two 5.25mm jump rings.

**17** With 5.25mm jump rings, join an end of both of the chains you made in Step 2 to the bar portion of a toggle clasp {**FIG. 3**}. Slip the bar through the toggle on the book and enjoy!

> ➼ *tip*
>
> Instead of covering a book with beadwork, try using a beautiful brocade ribbon.

# Keeping a Journal

For me, keeping a journal is an incredibly valuable experience. Indeed, I would feel lost if I didn't keep one. I have several journals. The first is one that I use to write my thoughts down in the morning—just a page or two of what is happening in my life and how I feel about it. Artistic? Not at all. Valuable? Definitely.

My second primary journal is one that I use solely for beading ideas. This book and its projects were born in the pages of my beading journal. When I review the pages, I find it interesting when an idea appears over and over. It changes ever so slightly with each repetition until whatever problem I foresaw in its construction is worked out, and I sit down at my bead table and create the piece. I draw impossible things and think that someday they will come into being. I draw variations of the impossible things as well as my current pieces. I write down experiments with materials, and if those experiments don't work, I create other ideas to try. I have lists, such as my list of possible projects for this book. I write down dreams when they stay with me upon waking and have a relevance to my work and life. I write quotes from books and draw the images that the words inspire. There are verses of poetry that spring into my mind.

I think my beading journal is beautiful, and part of its beauty lies in its value to me. When I don't sketch out an idea, it moves away from me and is forgotten. This journal has become more and more important to me.

I have the same fondness for a beautiful sketchbook as I do for beads, buttons, books, and ribbons. I have a couple of inspiration books filled with photos clipped from magazines. I have a large sketchbook where I draw ideas, coloring them with colored pencil and defining the detail with a fine-point marker. I use calligraphy to write about my ideas in this book. I have another large book into which I put more dreamlike work. I tear out images from magazines and write about big, intense projects that are more series-oriented than those in my beading journal. I clip photos of beautiful rooms and interesting ideas. And I must confess to having several more journals and sketchbooks that are still sitting on the shelf, empty and waiting.

When I first started to keep a journal on beading, I used a spiral-bound book that I originally used for ceramics. When I needed inspiration, I would take the sketchbook, a pencil, and eraser, a set of colored pencils, a fine-point permanent marker, and a few jewelry books with me to a coffee shop. I would sit for an hour, maybe two, and look through the books and then sketch out a few ideas and color them. I found that inspiration led to more inspiration. When I started to sketch my own ideas more often, I chose a different type of book—black hardbound—that I could keep in my purse.

# HINTS AND TIPS FOR JOURNALING

› Get a sketchbook that you enjoy working in. It doesn't have to be fancy or expensive—in fact, it's probably a good idea if it's not, because then you won't worry and edit what you put into it.

› Decide on your favorite sketching tools and be sure to buy enough. I like old-fashioned black Flair pens and the consistency of black line sketching throughout my book. If you like to use several colors of pens and want to add color, do so.

› Simplify your journal tool kit. If you need to take a lot of things with you to sketch, you're less likely to always have them with you. I have a sketchbook and my Flair pen, always.

› Once a week, take a book that inspires you, along with your sketchbook and pen, to a coffee shop. Tell yourself that you will make one sketch inspired by something in the book. Next time, do two. Don't tell yourself you'll make ten and then beat yourself up if you don't.

› Take just your sketchbook and pen to a coffee shop. Drink your coffee, look out the window, and let ideas come to you. Don't bring anything to inspire you. Don't beat yourself up if the ideas don't seem to be coming. If the ideas are slow, think about what sort of beaded bead you might like to do. Think of a beaded bottle and what sort of strange embellishment you might add to it. Design a necklace using these items. If someone is at the coffee shop wearing a beautiful necklace that you want to sketch, do it! Aren't you glad you brought your sketchbook?

› Cut out magazine pictures you find inspiring and glue them in a large sketchbook.

› Start a large journal that is devoted to more elaborate drawings, using color, collage, and written details. Choose a book with all-media paper so you can glue and paint in it.

# Washed Ashore

**FINISHED LENGTH:**
29" (73.5 cm)

There's nothing quite like a walk on the beach, searching for shells, jewels of sea glass, and a perfect piece of driftwood. When I hold these treasures in my hand, I wonder what story they hold inside them; how far had they traveled before I found them at the water's edge? In the *Washed Ashore* design, I wanted to bring elegance and a sense of refinement to a simple piece of worn wood by combining it with silk, pearls, chain, filigree, and beads. And now you have a good excuse to go to the beach to scout for treasures.

## MATERIALS

- ☐ Flat piece of driftwood, about 2½" × ¾" (6.5 × 2 cm)
- ☐ 1 brass or silver screw eye, 7⁄16" (1.2 cm)
- ☐ 1 piece of filigree that can be bent over the top of the driftwood
- ☐ E6000 adhesive
- ☐ 8 g size 15° seed beads in four or five colors (I used greens and brown)
- ☐ 5 g size 11° seed beads in three or four colors (greens and brown)
- ☐ 3 green or brown round beads, 4mm
- ☐ 1 piece of sea glass, thick enough to bead around
- ☐ Terrifically Tacky double-sided tape, ¼" (6 mm) wide
- ☐ 24 round Swarovski crystals, 2mm
- ☐ 47 to 50 jump rings, 5.25mm
- ☐ 6" (15.2 cm) of 24-gauge wire in gunmetal
- ☐ 1 yd (91.5 cm) Hannah silk cord

- ☐ 4.5 g cylinder beads in one color
- ☐ 16" (40.5 cm) brass chain with large links or a combination of large and small links
- ☐ 36 beads in an assortment of pearls, brass, and pressed glass
- ☐ 36 thin brass head pins with a ball at the end
- ☐ 24 daisy spacers, 3mm
- ☐ 24 crystals, 2mm
- ☐ 1 shank-style button, ¾" (2 cm) in diameter
- ☐ 8 fire-polished beads, 3mm
- ☐ 1 dagger bead
- ☐ 1 decorative jump ring, 9mm
- ☐ Beading thread of choice
- ☐ *Optional:* Gilder's paste
- ☐ *Optional:* Beeswax to condition thread

## TOOLS

- ☐ Small handheld drill
- ☐ Small round pointed file
- ☐ Size 12 beading needle
- ☐ Round-nose pliers
- ☐ Flat-nose pliers
- ☐ Flush cutters
- ☐ Small sharp scissors
- ☐ *Optional:* Size 13 beading needle

# TECHNIQUES

- Odd-count flat peyote stitch (20)
- Picot edge on peyote stitch (23)
- Zippering flat peyote stitch into a tube (24)
- Right-angle weave and embellishment (30)
- Basic wire wrap (40)
- Opening and closing a jump ring (41)
- Cranky wrap (41)
- Ribbon strap clasp (54)
- Freeform peyote stitch as instructed

**DRIFTWOOD DETAIL**

## STEPS

**1** Brush away any sand or debris that might be clinging to the piece of driftwood. Screw a ⁷⁄₁₆" (1.2 cm) screw eye into the top of the driftwood and then remove it.

**2** Fold a piece of brass filigree over the top of the driftwood, placing the hole in the filigree over the hole made by the screw eye.

**3** Dip the screw eye into E6000 adhesive and screw back into the hole you made in Step 1, holding the brass filigree in place. Let dry completely.

**4** If desired, lightly rub gilder's paste over the brass filigree with a piece of paper towel.

**5** Decide where you want to drill holes in the wood for beadwork and dangles. Mark with a pencil. Drill the holes using a small handheld drill and a very thin drill bit (see tip on page 103).

**6** To begin freeform peyote stitch, gather size 15° seed beads, size 11° seed beads, and 4mm round beads (I used a few different seaweed-colored greens). Although freeform peyote stitch typically uses a variety of beads, this piece is small, and too many types of beads will overwhelm it. The goal is just a hint of "seaweed" and a look of driftwood being dredged up from the water.

**7** Cut and condition a comfortable length of thread and thread a beading needle. Do not tie a knot or use a stop bead.

**8** Pass the needle and thread through a hole in the driftwood. I began in the top hole on the left side, planning to work my way down.

**9** Varying the size 15° seed beads with a few of the size 11° seed beads, string enough beads to go around the edge of the wood and back through the hole again. Tie a knot, leaving a 6" (15 cm) tail. Keep the loop that is going around the driftwood loose {**FIG. 1**}.

**10** String a variety of beads on the needle, work down to the next hole, and pass through it {**FIG. 2**}.

**11** String a variety of beads on the needle and loop around through another hole in the wood, or, to keep the thread in front, pass through one of the beads in the previous loop {**FIG. 3**}.

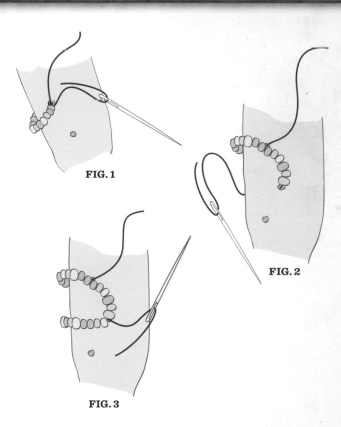

FIG. 1

FIG. 2

FIG. 3

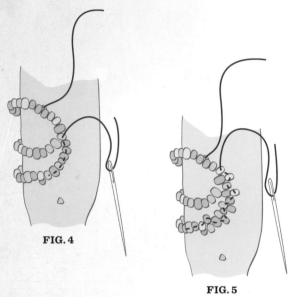

**FIG. 4**

**FIG. 5**

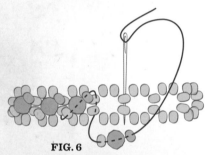

**FIG. 6**

**12** Work down to the next hole. String more beads on the needle and pass it through one of the beads in the front {**FIG. 4**}. Now you have the foundation for your seaweed.

**13** Start doing peyote stitch along the foundation on the front {**FIG. 5**}. Don't try to control the way it looks—simply do a few stitches, adding some beads here and there. Skip from one area to another by adding a variety of beads.

**14** Continue in peyote stitch until you're satisfied. This is freeform peyote, so stitch a bead in any direction you'd like to go. Stitch on top of the existing beadwork to create layers. You can't make a mistake here. Bring the thread to the back and fill in as needed. Tie off the working thread and the tail.

**15** Repeat the seaweed technique in the other holes you have made in the driftwood. Set aside.

**16** To bead the piece of sea glass, begin by cutting small pieces of double-sided tape and adhering them along the edge of the sea glass. Tape along the entire edge or skip space between pieces.

**17** With size 15° seed beads, make a strip of right-angle weave with 2 beads per side that will fit around the edge of the sea glass. Attach one end to the other with the last stitch.

**18** Embellish the right-angle weave with either 2mm round Swarovski crystals or size 11° seed beads {**FIG. 6**}.

**19** With size 15° seed beads, bring the needle and thread out of a set of 2 beads in the front {FIG. 7}.

**20** Changing to peyote stitch, stitch 1 bead in between each set of 2 beads all the way around. Step up by going through the first bead in this row {FIG. 8}.

**21** Stitch another row. Put on 1 bead the first stitch, 2 beads the second stitch, then 1 bead, then 2. Repeat around {FIG. 9}. Depending on the size and shape of the sea glass, you may need to vary the beads differently. Do a few stitches and you will be able to tell how the beadwork tightens around the front of the sea glass and how many beads to add.

**22** Pass the needle through the beads to the back of the piece and repeat Steps 20 and 21.

**23** Pass the needle through the beads to the top and reinforce the embellishment going across the right-angle weave. Switch to a size 13 needle if necessary.

**24** Sew a 5.25mm jump ring to the top of the sea glass. If the holes of the beads fill with thread, wiggle the needle under the beads and continue to reinforce the jump ring. Tie off the working thread and tail.

**25** With 24-gauge wire, bring one-third of the wire through the hole in the bottom of the driftwood. Make a wrap at the bottom {FIG. 10}.

**26** Make a wire wrap under the first one and use the rest of the wire for a cranky wrap.

**BEADED SEA GLASS**

**FIG. 7**

**FIG. 8**

**FIG. 9**

**FIG. 10**

**FIG. 11**

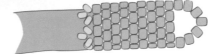

**FIG. 12**

**27** Carefully open the jump ring on the top of the sea glass and close through the loop at the bottom of the driftwood. The pendant is complete.

**28** To make the strap, cut a yard of Hannah silk cord into two 18" (45.5 cm) pieces.

**29** With cylinder beads, make a piece of odd-count peyote stitch long enough to wrap around one end of the silk cord (8 beads stacked on top of each other at the edge). Picot-edge one smooth side {**FIG. 11**}.

**30** Zipper the piece closed around one end of the silk cord. The edge without the picots should be at the end of the cord. Sew through the tube to secure the cord inside, being careful not to pull too tightly. With cylinder beads, make a loop of 7 beads at the bottom of the tube and reinforce {**FIG. 12**}.

**31** Repeat Steps 29 and 30 on the other cord.

**32** Knot one of the silk cords 1" (2.5 cm) from the top of the tube.

**33** Continue to make knots at 2" (5 cm) intervals and the last knot about a 1¼" (3.2 cm) interval. Do what looks best to you but keep in mind that knotting takes up quite a bit of the cord.

**BUTTON CLASP WITH BEADED TUBES**

**34** With 5.25mm jump rings, attach chain along the length of the cord, starting above the first knot and ending above the last knot {FIG. 13}. Do not cut the chain until after you have attached it.

**35** Repeat Steps 32 through 34 on the second piece of cord. Cut any excess chain.

**36** Wire-wrap a variety of pearls, glass beads, and brass beads. Attach the wire-wrapped beads to the chain on both straps using 5.25mm jump rings.

**37** With the silk cord, cylinder beads, size 15° beads, 3mm fire-polished beads, the dagger, and the button, make a Ribbon Strap Clasp.

**38** To complete the necklace, open a 9mm decorative jump ring and slip it through the screw eye on top of the pendant. Slip both loops at the bottom of each strap on to the jump ring, making sure the chain lies to the outside. Close the jump ring securely.

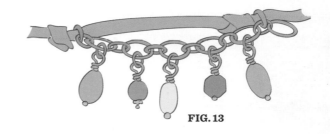

FIG. 13

SILK CORD WITH ATTACHED CHAIN AND BEADS

# Fairy Shrine

**FINISHED LENGTH:**
18½" (47 cm)

It's an especially fine thing when you not only recycle something but also end up with something sparkly and beautiful to wear. I'd wanted to do something with the plastic boxes that beads come in for a long time. As I looked for the perfect object to put in one of these boxes, I kept returning to a tiny Frozen Charlotte doll (a specific type of small molded doll without clothes). Each time I tried something else, I returned to the doll. This necklace is the result. I chose the materials as I went along, so I dedicate this shrine to flying by the seat of your pants, fairy dust included.

## MATERIALS

- ☐ Plastic container with flush lid, 1" × 2" × ¾" (2.5 × 5 × 2 cm) (you will not use the lid)
- ☐ 2" × 3" (5 × 7.5 cm) piece of cardstock
- ☐ Paper, collage, or photograph to fit inside the box
- ☐ Microscope slide
- ☐ Frozen Charlotte doll to fit in box
- ☐ Embellishments such as glitter, rhinestones, and lace to decorate the doll
- ☐ E6000 glue
- ☐ White glue
- ☐ 7.5 g cylinder beads in one color
- ☐ 2 g each of size 15° seed beads in two colors
- ☐ ¼" (6 mm) copper-foiling tape (enough to encircle microscope slide)
- ☐ Terrifically Tacky double-sided tapes, ½" (1.3 cm) and ¼" (6 mm) wide

- ☐ 75 round crystals, 2mm (or substitute size 11° seed beads)
- ☐ 12" (30.5 cm) of ⅛" (2 mm) wide silk ribbon
- ☐ Quartz crystal, stick pearl, or small twig
- ☐ Brass filigree for bail
- ☐ 6" (15 cm) rhinestone chain
- ☐ 18" (45.5 cm) of 4mm rubber cord or thin tubing
- ☐ 36" × 1" (91.5 × 2.5 cm) cross-grain strip of douppioni silk fabric
- ☐ 1 shank-style button, ¾" (2 cm) diameter
- ☐ 8 fire-polished beads, 3mm
- ☐ 1 dagger bead
- ☐ Beading thread of choice
- ☐ *Optional:* Beeswax to condition thread
- ☐ *Optional:* Head pins and 2.5mm, 3mm, or 4mm crystals (if the filigree has loops for hanging beads)

## TOOLS

- ☐ Utility knife
- ☐ Metal ruler with cork backing
- ☐ Glass cutter
- ☐ Size 12 beading needles
- ☐ Fine-point permanent marker
- ☐ Pencil
- ☐ Cotton swabs
- ☐ Bone folder
- ☐ 2 pairs of flat-nose pliers
- ☐ Round-nose pliers

## TECHNIQUES

▹ Odd-count flat peyote stitch (20)

▹ Picot edge on peyote stitch (23)

▹ Zippering flat peyote stitch into a tube (24)

▹ Even-count tubular peyote stitch (25)

▹ Tubular netting (36)

▹ Basic wire wrap (40)

▹ Foiling (42)

▹ Ribbon strap clasp (54)

### STEPS

*Note: Decorate the doll and glue all of the elements inside the box before you put on the glass. Work on the strip of peyote-stitch beadwork while the glue is drying.*

**1** This project uses a small plastic box of the type that beads are often sold in. Discard the lid. Make a view guide by tracing the box-lining template on page 111 on a piece of cardstock. Use a utility knife to cut out the shape. Hold the open area on the cardstock over a picture or collage to help with placement. Place the doll in the center to see how it will look inside your box.

**2** Measure the microscope slide to fit the front of the box, measuring from the very front, which is indented slightly from the sides and is slightly smaller than the back of the box. Cut the slide to fit using a glass cutter.

**3** Use the view guide to determine what will line the box and place the doll on top for further guidance {**FIG. 1**}.

**4** Place the box-lining template that you made in Step 1 over the paper or picture, trace the shape outline with a pencil, and cut out carefully, just inside the lines.

**5** Decorate the doll. Use E6000 adhesive to attach rhinestones and white glue to attach glitter.

**6** Fold the flaps of the box lining in and test the lining inside the box before you apply any glue. Trim edges if necessary to make the lining fit. Squeeze a few drops of white glue inside the box and spread evenly to the edges with a cotton swab.

**7** Carefully lay the paper inside and burnish with a clean cotton swab, wiping away excess glue.

**8** Glue a picture or collage on the back of the box using white glue, spreading it evenly to the edges with a cotton swab.

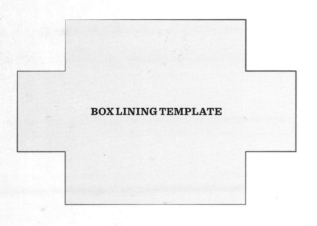

BOX LINING TEMPLATE

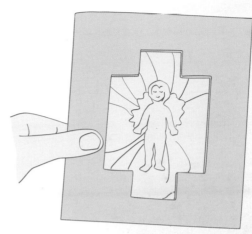

**9** Put E6000 adhesive on the back of the Frozen Charlotte doll and place it inside the box, pressing it firmly in place. Set aside and let dry.

**10** Make a strip of peyote-stitch beadwork that is 9 beads wide and 184 rows long, or 92 beads along the edge. You may need more or fewer rows, depending on your tension and how much you stretch the beadwork when putting it around the box.

**11** With size 15º seed beads, make a picot edge on both long sides of the strip, using one color for one side and a second color for the other {**FIG. 2**}.

**12** Clean the glass that you cut in Step 2. The inside should be clean and free of lint. Place on top of the box.

**13** With ¼" (6 mm) copper-foil tape, tape around the top portion of the box, placing the edge of the tape along the seam between the lid and box. Burnish along the sides with a bone folder.

**14** Fold the edges of the copper-foil tape over the glass, folding in the corners. Burnish well.

**15** Place ¼" (6 mm) double-sided tape around the edge of the box over the copper tape but do not fold over and do not peel away plastic coating.

**16** Place ½" (1.3 cm) double-sided tape along the sides of the box. Peel away the plastic and place the peyote-stitch strip on the tape, aligning the edge (the picots in back should extend out slightly from the top edge of the outer sides of the box) and pressing down firmly {**FIG. 3**}.

**17** Add rows of beadwork to the peyote-stitch strip if necessary. Zipper the edges together into a tube.

**18** Make a row of netting along the edge of the back of the box, skipping a picot and using a combination of size 15° seed beads and 2mm round crystals.

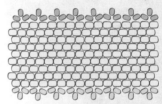

FIG. 2

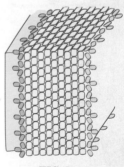

FIG. 3

**19** Sew 2mm round crystals on the front edge of the picots by sewing a crystal between each picot {**FIG. 4**}.

**20** Place a piece of ¼" (6 mm) wide double-sided tape around the quartz crystal, stick pearl, or small twig. Cut a length of beading thread and thread a needle. Place an even number of cylinder beads on the thread and tie around the crystal, pearl, or twig just outside the tape.

**21** Make enough even-count tubular peyote stitch to cover the tape. Make a row of size 15° seed beads at each end {**FIG. 5**}.

**22** Bend a piece of brass filigree into a bail shape and sew its front and back to the beadwork.

**23** If the filigree has loops for hanging beads, wire-wrap an appropriate number of crystals and attach to the filigree with jump rings. Sew the bail to the box, centering it at the top. Sew in two places so the box doesn't turn. Reinforce well.

**24** Press the double-sided tape at the top of the copper tape on the top of the box and then peel the plastic away.

**25** On the sides of the box, place a length of ⅛" (2 mm) silk ribbon along the tape starting at the center top. Tie a bow at the center bottom of the box. Trim away excess.

**26** Measure and cut pieces of rhinestone chain to fit the box's top, bottom, and sides along the front. Carefully put a thin layer of E6000 adhesive on top of the double-sided tape (where the copper foil is folded over the top of the glass). Place the rhinestone chain over the glue, pressing down gently and lining the chain up evenly. Remove excess glue with tweezers and a toothpick. Set aside and let dry.

**27** To make the strap, cut an 18" (45.5 cm) length of 4mm rubber cord or tubing. Starting at one end of the cord, wrap the 1" × 36" (2.5 × 91.5 cm) strip of silk tightly around it, overlapping the edges and making sure no rubber cord is showing. Allow the edges of the silk to fray.

**28** Using a knotted double thread, make a few stitches to secure the silk at the end of the cord. Wrap the thread over the silk several times and make a few more stitches. Tie off thread. Repeat at the other end of cord.

**29** Use the silk-covered tube, cylinder beads, size 15° beads, button, and 3mm fire-polished beads to make a Ribbon Strap Clasp.

**30** Put the strap through the bail to complete the necklace.

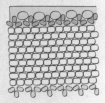

**FIG. 4**

**FIG. 5**

**FAIRY SHRINE VARIATION**

A pink and green colorway adds
a girly flavor to the Fairy Shrine.

# *Lavaliere*

**FINISHED LENGTH:**
20½" (52 cm)

A lavaliere is a pendant with a large drop, normally worn on a chain, popular in France in the Louis XIV era. For my version of this extravagant necklace, I alternated between bead-embroidered links and embellished ribbons. You may want to put your beautiful lavaliere on a chain to be true to the original style. This piece is worthy of an evening gown, but don't let that stop you from dressing up a pair of jeans.

## MATERIALS

- ☐ 1 square, oval, or round cabochon, about 20x30mm
- ☐ Beading foundation
- ☐ E6000 glue or Terrifically Tacky ¼" (6 mm) wide double-sided tape (see Note)
- ☐ 15 g size 15° seed beads in two or three colors
- ☐ 5 center-drilled coin pearls, 10mm
- ☐ 3 g size 11° seed beads
- ☐ 8 g cylinder beads in two colors
- ☐ 1 pearl for top of cabochon, 5 to 6mm
- ☐ 3" × 6" (7.5 × 15 cm) polyester suede fabric
- ☐ 6 decorative rings, 6mm
- ☐ 1 two-hole chandelier earring finding
- ☐ 36" (91.5 cm) 24-gauge wire
- ☐ 1 stone drop, about 18×25mm, top drilled
- ☐ 2 center-drilled coin pearls, 18mm

- ☐ 13 Japanese drops, 3.4mm
- ☐ Seed pearls with holes large enough for a size 13 needle
- ☐ ½ yd (45.5 cm) of ⅜" (1 cm) wide satin or velvet ribbon
- ☐ 2 horizontally drilled coin pearls, 10mm
- ☐ 4 bicone crystals, 4mm
- ☐ 19 jump rings, 8mm
- ☐ 12 daisy spacers, 3mm
- ☐ 1 toggle clasp, ¾" (2 cm)
- ☐ 36" (91.5 cm) of ⅛" (2 mm) wide rayon ribbon for tying between links
- ☐ Beading thread of choice
- ☐ *Optional:* Beeswax to condition thread

## TOOLS

- ☐ Beading needles, sizes 12 and 13
- ☐ Small sharp scissors
- ☐ Pencil
- ☐ Flush cutters
- ☐ Round-nose pliers
- ☐ 2 pairs of flat-nose pliers
- ☐ *Optional:* Permanent marker to color beading foundation

## TECHNIQUES

- ➤ Odd-count flat peyote stitch (20)
- ➤ Decrease in peyote stitch (22)
- ➤ Picot edge on peyote stitch (23)
- ➤ Even-count tubular peyote stitch (25)
- ➤ Tubular netting (36)
- ➤ Basic wire wrap (40)
- ➤ Opening and closing jump rings (41)
- ➤ Beaded cabochon with backstitch and picot edge (43)
- ➤ Ribbon link (52)

### STEPS

*Note: I used a vintage glass reverse-painted cabochon. If you use a similar cabochon, use glue to attach it to a piece of beading foundation instead of using double-sided tape. The tape has a tendency to lift away from the cab and remove paint along with it.*

**1** Glue or tape the 20×30mm cabochon to a piece of beading foundation. With size 15° seed beads, make a row of backstitch around the cabochon.

**2** Continuing with size 15° seed beads and using the row of backstitch as a base row, make a few rows of peyote stitch around the cabochon until the peyote stitch rises above the top of the cabochon.

**3** Depending on the shape of the cabochon, make a row of peaks (skip every other stitch) or put on 3 beads, skip an up-bead, and go through the next up-bead, all the way around. The beadwork should close around the top of the cabochon.

**4** Put a piece of double-sided tape or glue on the back side of the 10mm coin pearl and place it under the main cabochon, centering it and leaving 1 bead space between the pearl and the main cabochon. If using a pearl, sew it to the foundation and reinforce.

**5** Make a row of backstitch and a peyote-stitch bezel around the pearl.

**6** With size 11° seed beads, make a row of backstitch around the main cabochon and the pearl. With cylinder beads, make another row of backstitch around the main cabochon and the pearl.

**7** Sew the 5 to 6mm pearl at the top of the pendant, centering it and leaving a space large enough to backstitch with size 15° seed beads around it. Make a backstitch row around the pearl.

**8** Working on the wrong side of the piece to avoid cutting the stitches, carefully trim away the excess foundation with a pair of small

FIG. 1

RIBBON LINK

sharp scissors. Color the edge of the remaining foundation with a permanent marker if desired.

**9** Put a small amount of glue or double-sided tape on the wrong side of the beadwork and adhere it to the polyester suede fabric. Trim the fabric with the scissors to the edge of the foundation.

**10** Decide where the decorative rings should be placed at each top corner and lightly mark with a pencil. Decide where the chandelier earring finding will go at the bottom and lightly mark.

**11** Begin a picot edge around the piece. When you arrive at the pencil marks, sew on the rings and the chandelier earring finding. Resume the picot edge after sewing. Be sure to bring the needle through both the beading foundation and the polyester suede fabric as you picot. Set beadwork aside.

**12** With 24-gauge wire, wire-wrap the top of the stone drop and continue to wrap until the

holes of the drop are covered with wire. Place small pieces of double-sided tape in 4 places around the top of the drop.

**13** Using size 15° seed beads, string on an even number of beads that will go around the drop under the wire. Tie the beads in a circle around the drop.

**14** Stitch a couple of rows of tubular peyote stitch around the drop, adding 2 beads when a bead space is too large for 1 bead.

**15** Change to tubular netting, starting out with 3-bead netting. As the drop increases, go to 5-bead netting. Do 4 rows. On the last row, if using seed pearls, alternate a 3.4mm drop and a seed pearl for the center seed bead all the way around. Tie off thread.

**16** Open a jump ring, slip on the drop and bottom loop of the chandelier part, and close the jump ring tightly. Set aside.

**17** Make 4 flat Ribbon Links {**FIG. 1**}.

**BEADED CABOCHON DETAIL**

**18** Cut a rectangular piece of beading foundation and glue or tape an 18mm pearl or cabochon in the center. If using a pearl, sew the pearl down and reinforce.

**19** With size 15° seed beads, make a row of backstitch around the pearl and make a peyote-stitched bezel from this row.

**20** Glue or tape a pearl below the center pearl or cabochon, leaving a space of 1 bead between them. If using a pearl, sew down and reinforce.

**21** Make a row of backstitch around the pearl or cabochon and make a peyote-stitch bezel from this row.

**22** Glue or tape a pearl or cab above the center pearl, leaving a space of 1 bead between them. If using a pearl, sew down and reinforce.

**23** Using size 15° seed beads, make a row of backstitch around the pearl and make a peyote-stitched bezel.

**24** Using a different color of size 15° seed beads, do a row of backstitch around all 3 pearls. Trim the foundation, working from the wrong side to avoid cutting stitches. Color the edge of the foundation with a permanent marker if desired.

**25** Place a small piece of double-sided tape on the back of the link and press a piece of polyester suede fabric to the back. Let dry. Trim the fabric to the edge of the foundation.

**26** With a pencil, lightly mark the locations for the decorative rings at each end of each link.

**27** With size 15° seed beads, make a picot edge all around the link, sewing in the rings where you have marked them and then resuming the picots. Be sure to bring the needle through both the foundation and the fabric as you picot {FIGS. 2 AND 3}.

**28** Join the components. Use 2 jump rings per link and close them smoothly and tightly. The links will be less likely to flip around with 2 jump rings {FIG. 4}.

**29** At the end of each strap, make a wire wrap using 24-gauge wire with a coin pearl, a 3mm daisy spacer, and a 4mm bicone crystal on each side.

**30** Attach one half of the toggle clasp to each end of the wire wrap using jump rings.

**31** Cut a 3" (7.5 cm) length of narrow rayon ribbon and thread through a jump ring, tie in the back, bring to the front, and tie again. Repeat on each jump ring except for those connecting to the clasp. Alternate the colors of the ribbon or use the same color throughout. The project is complete.

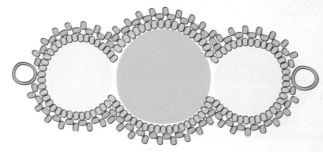

**FIG. 2**

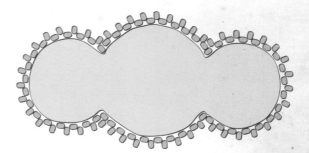

**FIG. 3**

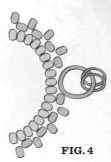

**FIG. 4**

LINKED COMPONENTS

# An Extra Pair of Hands

**FINISHED LENGTH:**
20" (51 cm)

Who couldn't use an extra pair of hands? I had planned for some time on making jewelry or sculpture using a pair of porcelain doll hands that had been in my stash for several years. When I began to write this book, out came the hands. Although this might be a rather strange piece of jewelry, I like the surprise and humor the hands bring to an otherwise serious piece. Now if I could only teach them how to dust.

## MATERIALS

- ☐ 1 pair of porcelain, china, or plastic doll hands
- ☐ Terrifically Tacky double-sided tape, ¼" (6 mm) wide
- ☐ 15 g cylinder beads in two colors
- ☐ 8 g size 15° seed beads in four to five colors
- ☐ 5 g Japanese drops, 3.4mm, in two colors
- ☐ 3 dagger beads, 3x10mm, in each of two colors
- ☐ 27" (68.5 cm) of ⅝" (1.5 cm) wide velvet or satin ribbon
- ☐ 2 round or oval cabochons, 18mm
- ☐ 4" × 4" (10 × 10 cm) beading foundation
- ☐ 10 g size 11° Japanese seed beads in two colors
- ☐ 2 pieces of 2" × 2" (5 × 5 cm) polyester suede fabric, to back cabochons

- ☐ ¾" × 8" (2 × 20.5 cm) strip of cotton fabric
- ☐ 1 shank-type button, 1" (2.5 cm) diameter or smaller
- ☐ 1 octagonal chandelier part, about 18mm wide
- ☐ 8" (20.5 cm) 24-gauge gunmetal wire
- ☐ 6" (15 cm) of ⅛" (3 mm) wide rayon ribbon
- ☐ 12" (30.5 cm) of ⅜" (1 cm) wide velvet or satin ribbon
- ☐ 4 brass triangle findings or round parts of toggle clasps, 12mm
- ☐ 90 to 100 fire-polished beads, 3mm
- ☐ 6 jump rings, 6mm and 9mm
- ☐ Beading thread of choice
- ☐ Sewing thread
- ☐ *Optional:* Beeswax to condition thread

## TOOLS

- ☐ Size 12 beading needles
- ☐ Plastic thread bobbin
- ☐ Small sharp scissors
- ☐ Handsewing needle
- ☐ Flush cutters
- ☐ Round-nose pliers
- ☐ Flat-nose pliers

# TECHNIQUES

> Odd-count flat peyote stitch (20)

> Decrease in odd-count peyote stitch (22)

> Picot edge on peyote stitch (23)

> Zippering flat peyote stitch into a tube (24)

> Even-count tubular peyote stitch (25)

> Tubular netting (36)

> Spiral rope (38)

> Basic wire wrap (40)

> Opening and closing a jump ring (41)

> Beaded cabochon with backstitch and picot edge (43)

HANDS DETAIL

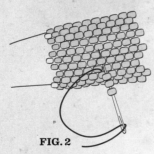

FIG. 1

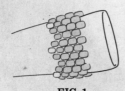

FIG. 2

FIG. 3

## STEPS

**1** Begin with the doll arms. Place a piece of double-sided tape around the top of a doll arm.

**2** Cut and condition a comfortable length of thread. Thread needle. Place an even number of cylinder beads on the thread to fit around the taped doll arm. Take the protective plastic off the double-sided tape and tie the beads around the doll arm on top of the tape. Leave an 8" (20.5 cm) tail.

**3** Without adding a bead, pass the needle through the first bead. You will be working toward the hand for a few rows and will then complete the top portion.

**4** Complete a few rows in peyote stitch, covering the double-sided tape and stepping up at the end of each row.

**5** With size 15° Japanese seed beads, complete 2 more rows. Because the doll arm tapers, changing to size 15° beads will close the beadwork around the arm.

**6** With size 15° beads in another color, make peaks along the bottom edge by skipping every other stitch {**FIG. 1**}.

**7** Bring the needle to the top of the beading on the arm by passing the needle through the beads. Peyote-stitch around the top of the doll arm using the same cylinders you started with, until you have beaded ½" (1.3 cm) past the top of the doll arm. Be sure to do the step-up at the end of each row. End with peaks by skipping every other stitch. Tie off the tail by weaving it around in the beadwork.

**8** Weave the working thread to about where the arm ends inside the peyote tube. With size 15° Japanese seed beads, put 3 beads on the needle, skip a bead space, and pass the needle through the next bead {**FIG. 2**}. Repeat all the way around and step up to begin the netting.

**9** Stitch enough rows of tubular netting to reach the bottom of the sleeve where the beads change to size 15° beads {**FIG. 3**}.

**10** On the last row, string 1 bead, pass through a bead on the last row of cylinders, string 1 bead and go through the center bead on the last row of netting. Do this all the way around to attach the netting to the sleeve {FIG. 4}.

**11** Bring the thread out of one of the center beads on the first row of netting. Create a second layer with two different colors of size 15° seed beads. Put on 2A, 1B, and 2A and pass the needle through the next center bead of the first row {FIG. 5}. You are creating a second layer. Repeat all the way around and step up.

**12** Stitch another row, but change the color of the center bead (color C) {FIG. 6}.

**13** Bead a third row, changing the center color again and changing the count to 3A, 1D, 3A {FIG. 7}. Step up.

**14** Bead a fourth row. Replace the center bead with a Japanese 3.4mm drop. Alternate between two colors if you wish {FIG. 8}.

**15** Work the thread up a few rows in the cylinders, above the netting {FIG. 9}. Embellish the top row of netting with size 15° seed beads and small dagger beads {FIG. 10}.

**16** If there is thread remaining, work up to one of the peaks in the top and wind the thread around a bobbin for later use. You can use this thread to attach the strap inside the sleeve.

**17** Repeat Steps 1 through 16 for the second hand.

**18** To make the long middle Ribbon Link, cut a piece of velvet or satin ribbon 27" (68.5 cm) long. Double the ribbon. Sew the ends together with a few stitches. Knot and cut thread.

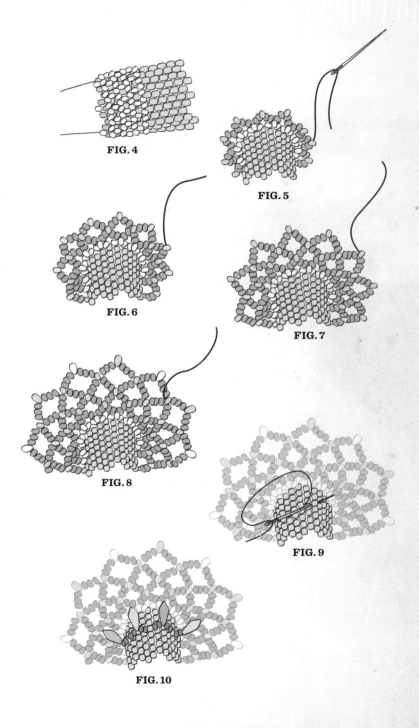

FIG. 4

FIG. 5

FIG. 6

FIG. 7

FIG. 8

FIG. 9

FIG. 10

**19** With cylinder beads, make two pieces of odd-count flat peyote stitch the width of the ribbon. Stitch 19 rows. The beads can be a different color than those you used on the doll arms. Decrease each end to a point. Picot the straight sides with size 15° seed beads.

**20** Attach the peyote piece to one end of the ribbon. Set the other piece aside until all of the picot edging is completed on both sides of the ribbon. Fold the beadwork over the end of the ribbon and stitch to the ribbon, starting at the point, to hold it in place. At the point, put 1 size 15° seed bead, one 3.4mm drop, and 1 seed bead. Sew again to reinforce. Bring the needle to the point on the other side of the ribbon and sew a drop on that point.

**21** Bring the needle to a center bead at the top and make a small loop of either cylinders or size 15° seed beads. Use an odd number of beads. My loop consists of 9 cylinder beads.

**22** Stitch a picot edge on both sides of the ribbon, catching both pieces in each stitch. When you finish one side, turn the ribbon over and start the other side at the same end you started the first side. If you don't start the picots at the same end, you will end up with a pucker. *Note:* When you do the picot edges, the ribbon will stretch somewhat, and the ends of the ribbon may not meet when you finish. If necessary, take out the stitches from Step 1 where you tacked the ends of the ribbon together. Trim the ends before you attach the peyote-stitch end cap.

**23** When both sides of the ribbon have a picot edge, sew on the other beadwork piece as in Steps 20 and 21.

**24** Make the beaded cabochon links. Cut two pieces of beading foundation larger than the cabochons. If you wish, dye or color the beading foundation and let dry. Glue or tape the cabochons to the squares.

**25** With size 15° seed beads, make a row of backstitch around a cabochon {**FIG. 11**}.

**26** Continuing with size 15° seed beads, using the row of backstitch as a base row, peyote-stitch around the cabochon, making a bezel, until the beading extends slightly over the top of the cabochon.

**27** When the bezel is built to the height that suits you, make peaks along the top edge by putting on a bead every other stitch, passing through the beads without adding a bead in between. This should tighten the beadwork over the edge of the cabochon {**FIG. 12**}.

**28** Using size 11° seed beads, stitch a row of backstitch next to the first row. Bring the working thread to the underside. With small sharp scissors, trim the beading foundation to the edge so it doesn't show, turning the piece over as you trim to avoid cutting the stitches. If you did not dye or color the foundation, color its edge with a permanent marker using a similar color to the size 15° seed beads you will use for the picot edge.

**29** Put a spot of glue or double-sided tape on the back of the cabochon and place a square of polyester suede fabric on top. Trim the suede to the edge of the beading foundation.

**30** With size 15° seed beads, make a picot edge all around the cabochon, sewing the suede fabric and beading foundation together.

FIG. 11

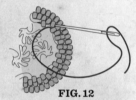

FIG. 12

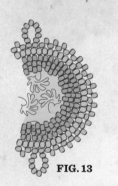

FIG. 13

With size 15° seed beads, make loops of 11 beads at the top and the bottom of the cabochon, being sure to center them {FIG. 13}.

**31** Repeat these steps for the second cabochon.

**32** To make the button and fabric link, begin by making a strip of peyote stitch 7 to 9 beads wide, depending on the size of the button {FIG. 14}.

**33** Bead about 12 rows (6 beads stacked up the side), then begin a window or hole for the shank of the button to fit into. To make the hole, the center bead should be a down-bead. Bead one side of the work until you have 4 beads stacked on top of each other on the inside and the inner top bead is a down-bead. Needle over to the other side and do the same {FIG. 15}.

**34** Put a bead in the center to close the top of the window and then needle over to the end {FIG. 16}. Do not put any beads on as you needle over to the end, or the row will have a step-down, and the center bead will not turn out correctly.

**35** Resume peyote stitch until you have the same amount of beadwork on both sides.

**36** Make peaks (Decrease in Odd-Count Peyote Stitch, page 22) at both ends and picot both sides {FIG. 17}.

**37** Cut a strip of fabric ¾" × 8" (2 × 20.5 cm). With a handsewing needle and sewing thread, baste with running stitches along one long edge.

**38** Pull up the thread to gather the fabric into a circle and attach the ends with a few

RIBBON LINK AND BEADED CABOCHON

FIG. 14

FIG. 15

FIG. 16

FIG. 17

stitches. Knot and cut thread. On the peyote beadwork piece that you made earlier, pass the thread down to one of the middle beads in the side of the window. Slip the shank of the button through the hole in the center of the fabric circle and then place it inside the window in the peyote-stitch piece. Sew the button shank inside the window, placing a bead inside the shank and reinforcing well.

**39** Add a loop of cylinder beads or size 15° seed beads or sew a jump ring at each end.

**40** For the octagonal chandelier link, begin by cutting two 4" (10 cm) lengths of 24-gauge wire. Bend one of the wires in the middle and slip into the top hole of the chandelier part. Bring the wire together at the top and make a wire wrap using both ends. With the second wire, make a wire wrap at the bottom of the chandelier part.

**41** Cut two 2" (5 cm) lengths of thin rayon ribbon (or torn fabric strips). Tie one of the ribbons over the top wire wrap in the back. Bring the ribbon ends around to the front and tie again. Trim the ends if the ribbon is too long.

**42** Repeat with the second ribbon, tying it over the bottom wire wrap.

NIPPED-WAIST RIBBON LINKS

**43** For the nipped-waist ribbon link, cut a length of ribbon about 6" (15 cm) long. Slip 2 brass triangles onto the ribbon and bring the ends of the ribbon to the center, wrong sides together, and attach the ends with a few stitches. Sew together and sew through the ribbon layers with a triangle at each end.

**44** With cylinder beads, bead a piece of peyote stitch 11 beads wide and long enough to wrap around the middle of the ribbon. Picot the sides. Size it so that the ribbon scrunches in when the peyote piece is zippered closed. After closing, sew through the tube down the length, back and forth to secure it to the ribbon {FIG. 18}. Repeat for the second link.

**45** Join all the links you have made using 2 or 3 jump rings, depending on how big your loops are. More than one jump ring will help keep the links facing forward.

**46** Make the spiral rope. Gather two colors of size 11° Japanese seed beads and two colors of 3.4mm Japanese drops. Cut and condition a comfortable length of thread and thread a beading needle. Put a stop bead at the end, leaving an 8" (20.5 cm) tail.

**47** String 4A and 3B. Push the beads next to the stop bead.

**48** Pass through the 4 beads of color A again {FIG. 19}.

**49** String 1A bead, 1B bead, 1 drop, and 1B bead. Pass through 4 color A beads again {FIG. 20}.

**50** String 1A bead and 3B beads. Pass through 4 color A again {FIG. 21}.

**51** Repeat Steps 49 and 50 until the strand measures 5" (12.5 cm). Make a loop of 7 size 11° seed beads to finish.

**52** Repeat Steps 46 through 51 to make a second strand.

**53** Attach the doll hands and straps. With color A size 11° seed beads, make a loop of 7 beads at the very end of the spiral rope. Reinforce well, tie off thread, and set aside.

**54** Stitch a 3mm fire-polished glass bead between the peaks of each of the doll hands. Put on one 3mm fire-polished bead and pass the needle from peak to peak. Go through twice.

**55** Thread the tail thread from one of the spiral ropes on a needle and pass the needle through the beadwork on a doll arm, a few rows down from the top of the doll arm. The spiral rope should slip inside just a bit. Tie off the thread, hiding it in the cylinder beads.

**56** With color B of size 11° seed beads, sew from the 3mm fire-polished beads to the spiral rope, going all the way around a few times, putting on a bead or two and going back and forth from the rope to the fire-polish bead {FIG. 22}. Reinforce well.

**57** Open a 9mm jump ring, slip on the spiral rope and end of the brass triangle, and close tightly.

**58** Repeat from Step 53 with the second doll hand and spiral rope to complete the project.

➺ *tips*

If you can't find brass triangles, use the round parts of toggle clasps or metal rings.

If you have trouble sewing the peyote stitch closed around the ribbon, wrap sewing thread tightly around the center of the ribbon several times to scrunch in the waist. The peyote beadwork will be easier to close around the ribbon. This method is useful whenever you use a wide ribbon or a wide strip of torn fabric.

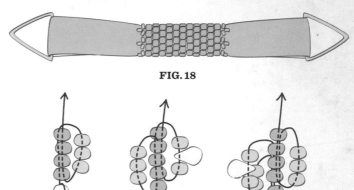

FIG. 18

FIG. 19   FIG. 20   FIG. 21

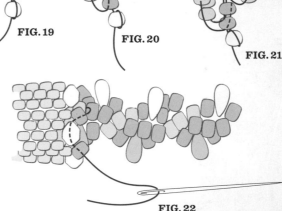

FIG. 22

# *Witch's Enchantment*

**FINISHED LENGTH:**
19" (48.5 cm),
pendant 9" (23 cm)

The idea of a witch conjures up many images: an old crone, torn rags for clothing, a ramshackle hut deep in the woods. Or a beautiful temptress with raven hair casting spells from her magical kitchen, replete with jars of mysterious ingredients. The *Witch's Enchantment* neckpiece is all of these: worn and torn, magical and mysterious, beautiful. The fibers, fabric, charms, and talismans you choose can cast any sort of spell. In the words of Glenda in *The Wizard of Oz,* "Are you a good witch or a bad witch?" Let's find out.

## MATERIALS

*For the neckpiece:*

- ☐ Assortment of ribbons, fibers, or fabric that has been torn or cut into strips
- ☐ 18 g cylinder beads in four or more colors
- ☐ 8 g size 15° Japanese seed beads in three or more colors
- ☐ 1 button, ¾" (2 cm) diameter
- ☐ 8 fire-polished beads, 3mm
- ☐ 1 dagger bead
- ☐ Craft plywood large enough for pendant shape
- ☐ Acrylic gesso
- ☐ 50 round crystals, 2mm
- ☐ 1 piece of brass filigree, about ⅝" × ⅝" (1.5 × 1.5cm)
- ☐ 2 brass daisy spacers, 4mm
- ☐ 1 brass head pin
- ☐ 1 brass or bronze filigree, about 1⅛" × 1⅛" (3 × 3cm)
- ☐ Watch face
- ☐ E6000 adhesive
- ☐ 3 decorative jump rings

- ☐ 2 pieces of chain, each 2½" (6.5 cm) long
- ☐ Decorative paper or collage materials
- ☐ Scissors
- ☐ Glue or matte medium

*For the charms and talismans:*

- ☐ 1 small bottle
- ☐ Brass filigree to wrap around bottle
- ☐ Brass prong setting
- ☐ Cameo to fit into setting
- ☐ 22-gauge wire to wrap the bottle
- ☐ 1 glass bead to thread onto wire
- ☐ E6000 adhesive
- ☐ Old key
- ☐ 1 piece of chain, 3" (7.5 cm) long
- ☐ 2 jump rings, 15mm
- ☐ 1 decorative jump ring, 10mm
- ☐ Beading thread of choice
- ☐ *Optional:* Beeswax to condition thread

## TOOLS

- ☐ Size 12 beading needle
- ☐ Pencil
- ☐ Oval template
- ☐ Dremel tool with sandpaper wheel and cutting blade
- ☐ Fine sandpaper
- ☐ Paper plate or palette for paints and matte medium
- ☐ Small sharp scissors
- ☐ Small handheld drill
- ☐ 2 pairs of flat-nose pliers
- ☐ Round-nose pliers
- ☐ Flush cutters
- ☐ Fine-tip permanent marker

## TECHNIQUES

- ➤ Odd-count flat peyote stitch (20)
- ➤ Picot edge on peyote stitch (23)
- ➤ Zippering flat peyote stitch into a tube (24)
- ➤ Stitch in the ditch (29)
- ➤ Right-angle weave and embellishment (30)
- ➤ Basic wire wrap (40)
- ➤ Opening and closing a jump ring (41)

FIBERS GATHERED INTO BEADED TUBES

### STEPS

**1** Begin with the neckpiece. Cut fibers and tear or cut fabric into strips (mine are about 19" [48.5 cm]). Cut a little longer than the desired length so you can trim the ends after sewing on beaded tubes. The fibers may slip a bit and will not be all the same length, so plan for this in advance and cut off any excess. Cut and condition a comfortable length of thread, tie a knot at the end, and thread a beading needle.

**2** Gather the fibers at one end, keeping the ends as close together as you can. Bring the needle through the fibers a few times and then start to wrap the thread around the fibers until you have about 6" (15 cm) of thread remaining. Be sure to catch all the fibers. Pass the needle through the wrapped area a few times, securing the fibers inside the wrap, and then knot and tie off the thread. Trim the ends of the fibers close to where the thread starts to wrap.

**3** With cylinder beads, make a strip of odd-count peyote 15 beads wide and long enough to wrap around the fibers at the thread-wound end. Add a picot edge of size 15° seed beads to one smooth edge of the strip of peyote (the other end will have a clasp). Zipper closed around the end of the fibers {**FIG. 1**}.

**4** Sew through the tube, back and forth, going through a bead to hide the thread, up and down a few times, ending with the thread at the top. Stitching in the ditch, start a second layer on top of the end tube 7 beads wide. The first row you bead stitching in the ditch will have 4 stitches. For the fourth stitch, loop under the thread and back through the bead. When it is long enough to wrap around the tube, picot both long, smooth sides. Zipper closed around the tube. String a loop of cylinder beads from one side of the tube end to the other and attach the button {**FIG. 2**}.

**5** Repeat Steps 2 through 4 at the other end of the ribbons and fibers. Attach a loop closure at the second end using cylinder beads, 3mm fire-polished beads, and a dagger bead in the center {**FIG. 3**}.

**6** To make the center bead, make a peyote stitch piece that is 21 cylinder beads wide and long enough to wrap around the fibers, or the same length you used for the ends. Picot both sides with size 15° seed beads before zippering. Zipper closed around the fibers. Make sure the tube is centered before you sew through it to secure the ribbons and fibers in place. Sew through the tube a few times, just enough to keep it in place. Stitching in the ditch, make a second layer that is 15 cylinder beads wide. Add a dot pattern in the second row from the edge if you wish. Picot the edges with size 15° seed beads and then zipper closed around the tube. Stitching in the ditch again, make a third layer that is 7 cylinder beads wide. I added a flower pattern in the center {FIG. 4}. Picot both edges with size 15° beads and zipper closed around tube.

**7** To make the in-between beads on either side of the center, make a beaded bead with a first layer that is 13 or 15 cylinder beads wide. Picot the sides with size 15° seed beads before zippering around fibers and sewing through the tube to attach it. Add a second layer that is 5 or 7 cylinder beads wide. Again, picot the sides with size 15° seed beads before zippering around the tube {FIG. 5}. The neckpiece now has a center bead, 2 in-between beaded beads, and end beads with clasp.

**8** Using cylinder beads, make 2 loops at the bottom of the center beaded bead. Slip two ½" (1.3 cm) lengths of chain onto a decorative jump ring and close inside the beaded loops {FIG. 6}.

**CENTER BEAD, VARIATION (PAGE 133)**

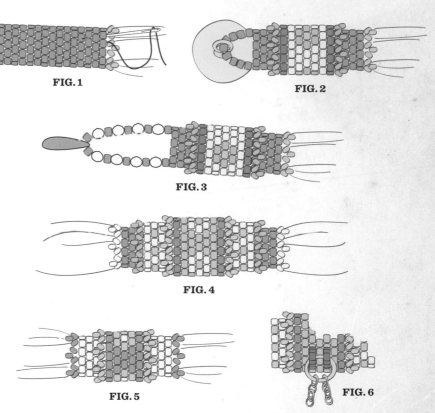

FIG. 1

FIG. 2

FIG. 3

FIG. 4

FIG. 5

FIG. 6

**PENDANT DETAIL**

**9** To begin the pendant and dangles, draw a shape on a piece of craft plywood with a pencil and an oval template. Roughly cut out with Dremel tool and cutting blade. Mine is an oval shape.

**10** Using a Dremel tool and sandpaper wheel, grind down to the pencil line.

**12** Using fine sandpaper, smooth and slightly round the edges and sand lightly over the top of the shape.

**13** Paint both sides of the shape with gesso and let dry. Lightly sand. The wood is now ready to paint or collage.

**14** To collage, cut out paper or collage material in the shape of the pendant. Use the template to make this easier.

**15** Using size 15° Japanese seed beads, make a row of right-angle weave around the edge of the pendant. Embellish with 2mm round crystals. Close the right-angle weave with a combination of the size 15° seed beads and cylinder beads. You may have to vary the number of beads per stitch to close over the edge {FIG. 7}.

**16** Using a drill, make a hole in the top and bottom center. Bend a piece of filigree and fit it over the top of the pendant, lining up the bottom holes in the filigree with the hole in the pendant. Thread a 4mm brass spacer onto a head pin and insert it into the bottom hole of the filigree and through the pendant. Place another 4mm spacer on the head pin and bend the head pin into a loop to hold the filigree {FIG. 8}. You may need to trim the head pin first.

**17** Put a 15mm jump ring through the hole at the bottom of the pendant and close it tightly.

**18** Glue the watch face to a piece of filigree with E6000 adhesive and glue the filigree to the front of the pendant. Trim the filigree if necessary.

**19** Bend a piece of filigree to the shape of the bottle and glue in place.

**20** Prepare the bottle. Cut the loop off the prong setting and file. Place the cameo inside and bend prongs to hold it securely. Glue the cameo unit to the bottle. Wire-wrap the top of the bottle. With jump rings, attach a 3" (7.5 cm) length of chain.

**21** Put jump rings on the filigree at the top of the pendant and attach to the chains on the strap.

**22** Open the jump ring at the bottom of the pendant, slip the chain attached to the bottle through it, and close the jump ring tightly. *Witch's Enchantment* is now complete . . . the spell has been cast.

**FIG. 7**

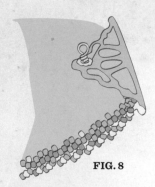

**FIG. 8**

## WITCH'S ENCHANTMENT VARIATION

The same components in a new colorway, with cranky-wrapped dangles and a feminine pendant, create a dramatically different mood.

# La Noblesse

**FINISHED LENGTH:**
7¼" (18.5 cm)

I enjoy treasure hunting at flea markets, antiques shops, and online. While browsing in an antiques shop in South Pasadena, California, I came across an antique shoe buckle that made a natural curve around the wrist and immediately thought of turning it into a bracelet. A strip of peyote stitch, ribbons, and beads provides a wonderful mix of old and new and an intriguing combination of textures. Wear *La Noblesse* with jeans or with a party dress to become Marie Antoinette for an evening.

## MATERIALS

- □ 4 g each of cylinder beads in four colors
- □ 6 g size 15° Japanese seed beads
- □ 2 drop beads
- □ Antique shoe buckle
- □ 12" to 14" (30.5 to 35.5 cm) of velvet ribbon in a width to match shoe buckle
- □ Terrifically Tacky double-sided tape, ½" (1.3 cm) wide
- □ 4 buttons, 2- or 4-hole, ½" to ¾" (1.3 to 2 cm) diameter
- □ 2 or 3 dagger beads, pressed-glass rings, or other beads for each button

- □ Assortment of charms
- □ 20 crystals and spacers, 3 to 4mm, to embellish centerpiece dangles
- □ 6" (15 cm) double-fold bias tape for edges of ribbon
- □ 2 snaps, size 2/0
- □ 36" (91.5 cm) of ⅛" to ¼" (3 to 6 mm) wide ribbon (or strips of fabric) to tie around button dangles
- □ Beading thread of choice
- □ Sewing thread
- □ *Optional:* Beeswax to condition thread

## TOOLS

- □ Size 12 beading needle
- □ Handsewing needle
- □ Small sharp scissors

## TECHNIQUES

> Odd-count flat peyote stitch (20)

> Decrease in odd-count peyote stitch (22)

> Picot edge on peyote stitch (23)

> Beaded fringe (35)

> Sewing snaps to beadwork (44)

DANGLES

FIG. 1

FIG. 2

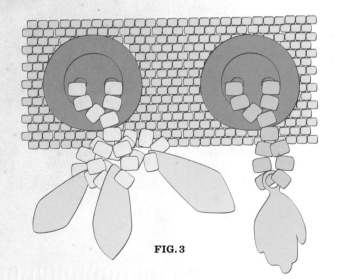

FIG. 3

## STEPS

**1** With cylinder beads, make a strip of peyote stitch 17 to 19 beads wide and 5" to 6" (12.5 to 15 cm) in length. You may need to adjust these measurements to fit the shoe buckle. The finished strip should be narrower than the velvet ribbon and should cover the open area in the center of the buckle.

**2** In peyote stitch, decrease each end to a point as shown in **FIG. 1**.

**3** Make a picot edge along each long side using size 15° Japanese seed beads. At the points of the beadwork, add 3 size 15° seed beads, a small drop, and 3 size 15° seed beads {**FIG. 2**}.

**4** Cut the velvet ribbon about 1½" (3.8 cm) longer than the strip of beadwork. The ribbon must be wider than the peyote stitch and should fit through the bar in back of the shoe buckle. Put 1" (2.5 cm) pieces of double-sided tape on the back of the peyote-stitch strip, at the center and both ends, to hold the beaded strip in place as you sew it to the ribbon. Press the peyote band onto the ribbon where you have put the tape. Curve the ribbon as you do this—this cuff should be curved, as making it flat will wrinkle the ribbon and place stress on the beadwork.

**5** Sew the beadwork to the ribbon, stitching between the second and last cylinder bead and sewing all the way around the beadwork, including the ends. Be sure to keep the curve. Place the shoe buckle in the center of the ribbon/beadwork band and secure it in place with a few stitches. If your buckle has no holes in the bar in back, go around the bar. Pull the thread through to the beadwork side, hide the thread in a few beads, and then go back through the ribbon. Knot and trim thread.

**6** Decide on selection and placement of buttons. Using doubled beading thread and a beading needle, sew a button on near the shoe buckle. Sew on daggers (I used 3) or dangles of your choice. Make a "stem" with seed beads between the button and the dangles.

**7** Repeat Step 6 three more times. I've used 2 buttons on one side with dangles and 1 button with a charm and 1 button with daggers on the other. Sew on the charm, again adding a stem of seed beads {FIG. 3}. Reinforce. If you prefer a symmetrical look, duplicate the dangles you've already made.

**8** With a doubled thread, sew a few dangles to the center portion of the opening in the buckle, centered or off-center: tie a knot or two at the end of the thread, go through the ribbon a few times, and then go through the ribbon and beadwork, coming out between the beads to add another dangle {FIG. 4}. Place a 3" to 4" (7.5 to 10 cm) strip of double-sided tape on the back of the piece, maintaining the curve.

BUCKLE DETAIL

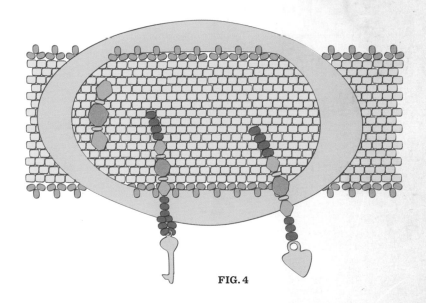

FIG. 4

**FIG. 5**

CLOSURE DETAIL

Place another piece of velvet ribbon along the back and trim to match the top piece. The wrong sides of the ribbon should face each other so you have the same beautiful velvet against your wrist.

**9** Cut a piece of bias tape ½" (1.3 cm) longer than the width of the ribbon. Fold ¼" (6 mm) on each end of the bias tape and sew to the end of the ribbon using a handsewing needle and thread. Repeat on the other end, making sure that the ribbon ends are well covered so the ribbon won't ravel. Push the ribbon up inside the bias tape as you go along—it has a tendency to slip out.

**10** With size 15° Japanese seed beads, make a picot edge along the long edges of the velvet ribbon. Make a picot on the inside ribbon only when you get to the bar in the shoe buckle. This is necessary to maintain the opening for the buckle between the two ribbons. Keep the curve. Sew 2 snaps to each end {FIG. 5}.

**11** Cut lengths of narrow ribbon or fabric strips about 3" (7.5 cm) long and tie one around each seed-bead stem that emerges from the buttons, as shown in the photographs.

## LA NOBLESSE VARIATION

This variation uses dazzling silver beads, hot pink velvet ribbon, and black charms for a stylish cuff.

# Norwegian Summer

**FINISHED LENGTH:**
8" (20.5 cm)

My husband, Asbjorn, grew up on a farm in Norway that has been in his family for more than 300 years. We were visiting for his niece Andrea's wedding when the mother of the bride asked us to go into the woods and pick flowers for a decoration. I had never seen so many lilies of the valley in bloom; the forest floor was covered with them. I designed this cuff to showcase this beautiful, delicate flower. This piece tells a part of my story, making it special. And Asbjorn says he can almost smell the flowers.

## MATERIALS

- ☐ Beading thread of choice
- ☐ *Optional:* Beeswax to condition thread

### For the Buttonhole Closure:

- ☐ 10 g light green size 11° Japanese seed beads
- ☐ 6 soldered jump rings
- ☐ 1 shank-style button, ¾" (2 cm) diameter

### For the Lily of the Valley Strand:

- ☐ 8" (20.5 cm) green rattail cord (more for large wrist)
- ☐ 15 g ivory size 15° Japanese seed beads
- ☐ 20–25 g white size 6° seed beads, crow beads, or 5mm round beads
- ☐ 2–3 g ivory size 11° seed beads
- ☐ 2 g pale yellow size 15° seed beads
- ☐ 2.5 g light green size 11° seed beads

### For the Ribbon Strand:

- ☐ 6" (15 cm) of ⅝" (1.5 cm) wide green velvet ribbon
- ☐ 6 eyelets, ⅛" (2 mm) diameter

- ☐ 6 oval jump rings
- ☐ 4 pressed glass flower spacers
- ☐ 4 glass or crystal beads, 8mm
- ☐ 4 bead caps
- ☐ 2 green spacer beads
- ☐ 2 green rondelle beads
- ☐ 4 white silk flowers 1" (2.5 cm) diameter
- ☐ 4 head pins

### For the Chain Strand:

- ☐ 8" (20.5 cm) chain (more for large wrist)
- ☐ 2 oval jump rings
- ☐ 6 gunmetal 10mm jump rings
- ☐ 6 green Lucite leaves with hole, about 1" (2.5 cm) wide

### For the Dangle:

- ☐ An assortment of rondelles, glass flowers, crystals, baroque crystal pendant, jump rings, 3mm crystals, and head pins

## TOOLS

- ☐ Size 12 beading needles
- ☐ 2 pairs of flat-nose pliers
- ☐ Round-nose pliers
- ☐ Flush cutters
- ☐ Scissors
- ☐ Eyelet-setting tool such as Crop-a-Dile

# TECHNIQUES

> Odd-count flat peyote stitch (20)
> Right-angle weave and embellishment (30)
> Zippering flat peyote stitch into a tube (24)
> Tubular netting (36)
> Basic wire wrap (40)
> Opening and closing a jump ring (41)

**BEADED CLASP**

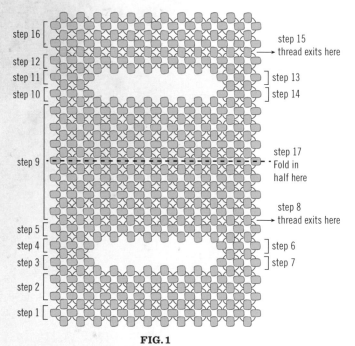

step 16
step 15
thread exits here
step 12
step 11
step 13
step 10
step 14

step 9
step 17
Fold in
half here

step 8
thread exits here

step 5
step 4
step 6
step 3
step 7

step 2

step 1

**FIG. 1**

## STEPS

**1** Begin with the right-angle-weave closure. With size 11° Japanese seed beads, make 12 stitches of right-angle weave.

**2** Stitch 2 more rows for a total of 3 rows of right-angle weave.

**3** Stitch a row with 2 stitches. Turn and stitch another row with just 2 stitches. Turn and stitch another row with 2 stitches. Continue this row with 10 more stitches, making a total of 12 stitches in the row.

**4** Make 2 stitches under the row to work down. Turn to start the next row and connect to the bottom with 2 stitches.

**5** Pass through the existing thread paths to exit the top end stitch. Stitch 7 rows.

**6** Stitch a row with 2 stitches. Turn and stitch another row with 2 stitches. Turn and stitch another row with 2 stitches. Continue this row with 10 more stitches, making a total of 12 stitches in the row.

**7** Make 2 stitches under the row to work down. Turn to start the next row and connect to the bottom with 2 stitches.

**8** Pass through the existing thread paths to exit the top end stitch. Stitch 2 more rows {**FIG. 1**}.

**9** Fold in half horizontally, lining up the beads on the sides and bottom and the buttonholes. Connect the edges, completing right-angle-weave stitches, stringing 1 bead and circling around. Connect the sides and bottom {**FIGS. 2 AND 3**}.

**10** Pass through the existing thread path to exit a bead along the inside hole. Connect the sides, top, and bottom. Do not connect the inside corner beads on all four corners.

**11** Sew 3 soldered jump rings along the bottom edge.

**12** Begin the button tab. Stitch 7 rows of right-angle weave, 12 stitches wide {**FIG. 4**}.

**13** Fold in half. Find the center 4 stitches. Stitch a new row of 4 stitches in right-angle weave over those 4 center stitches {**FIGS. 5 AND 6**}.

**14** Stitch a total of 7 rows {**FIG. 7**}.

**15** With right-angle weave, attach the end of this tab next to where it begins {**FIGS. 8 AND 9**}.

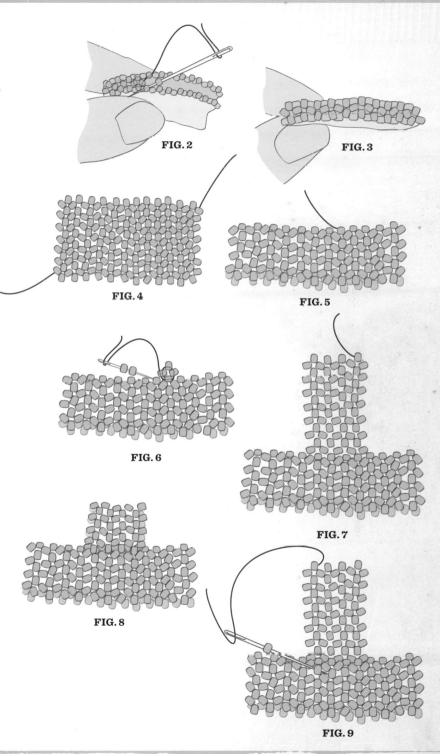

FIG. 2

FIG. 3

FIG. 4

FIG. 5

FIG. 6

FIG. 7

FIG. 8

FIG. 9

**16** Pass through the existing thread path to exit the top. With the same size 11° seed beads, string a loop of 7 beads to attach the button to the top {FIG. 10}. Work down and close one side, the bottom, and then the other side.

**17** Sew 3 soldered jump rings along the bottom edge.

**18** Begin the lily of the valley strand. Cut the rattail cord about 8" (20.5 cm) long. Cut a thread 20" (51 cm) long. Thread needle. You will not need a stop bead or a knot.

**19** String 6 ivory size 15° seed beads and tie in a circle leaving a tail of 8" (20.5 cm). Without putting a bead on, pass through the first bead.

**20** String 1 ivory size 15° seed bead, pass through the next bead 6 times, and step up through the first bead added in this step.

**21** String 3 beads and pass through the next bead of the previous round 6 times. Step up by passing through the first 2 beads added in this step {FIG. 11}. Repeat 5 times. Tie off thread.

**22** Put a needle on the tail. Pass down through the hole in the top of the flower. String 1 size 6° seed bead, 1 ivory size 11° seed bead, and 3 pale yellow size 15° seed beads.

**23** Pass back up through the size 11° seed bead and the size 6° seed bead. The size 15° seed beads should make a picot at the bottom.

**24** String 1 ivory size 11° seed bead, then 1, 2, or 3 green size 11° seed beads and stitch through the rattail cord. Make a stitch (pick up just a few threads to secure).

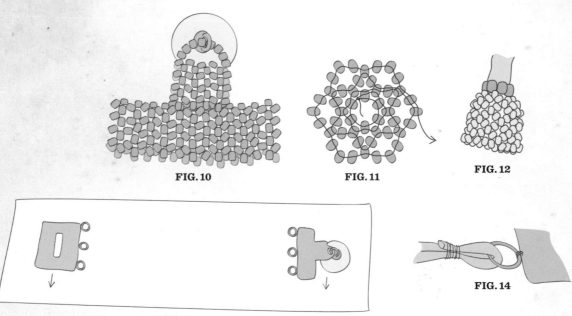

FIG. 10          FIG. 11          FIG. 12

FIG. 13          FIG. 14

**25** Pass back through the rattail, the green size 11° seed beads, and the ivory size 11° seed bead. Sew through a few of the size 15° seed beads in the flower and then tie off thread {FIG. 12}.

**26** Make 20 to 26 of the beaded flowers. Wait to sew on the last few until the strand is attached to the closure so you can fill in sparse areas and use 2 or 3 in the dangle.

**27** To determine the length of the strands: Measure A to B (your comfortable, desired length for the bracelet) for the total length of the bracelet {FIG. 13}.

**28** Measure from the set of jump rings on one end of the closure to the jump rings on the other side of the closure; that measurement is the length of the strands, including a lily of the valley strand, a chain with Lucite leaves, and a strand of velvet ribbon with eyelets and wire-wrapped silk flower components. In the finished bracelet, the strands cross. Plan your bracelet before attaching the strands.

**29** Attach the lily of the valley strand.

**30** Loop one end of the rattail cord through one of the jump rings.

**31** With a thread, doubled and knotted at the end, bring the sides of the rattail cord together, sew through a few times and wrap to secure {FIG. 14}. Tie off thread.

**32** With cylinder beads, stitch a strip of peyote that is 5 beads wide and long enough to wrap around the rattail cord where it is sewn together. Picot both long, smooth sides with ivory size 15° seed beads.

STRANDS AND CLASP

**33** Wrap the peyote piece around the rattail and zipper closed. Sew through the peyote tube a few times, going through the beads to hide the thread, and secure it to the cord. Tie off thread.

**34** Lay out the strand and have the closure to the appropriate measurement as we did in Step 28. Figure out the length of the strand (it may be slightly longer if you plan to cross it over another strand).

**35** Loop cord through the ring and repeat Steps 30 through 33.

**36** After sewing the other end of the cord and before trimming, try it on to be sure it's the correct length. You can always clip the thread and do it over if necessary. Wait until all the strands are attached before sewing on any remaining flowers.

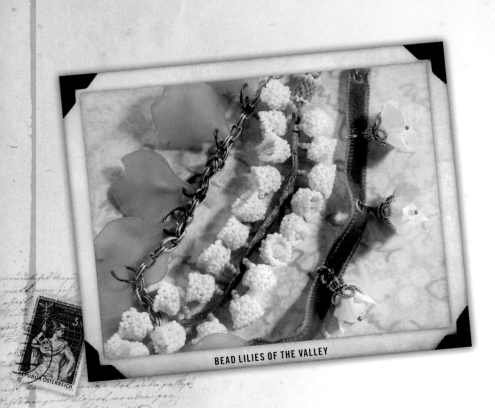

**BEAD LILIES OF THE VALLEY**

**37** Attach the chain strand. Open a jump ring and attach one end of the chain to one of the soldered rings. Measure and attach the other end of the chain. Wait until you are done with the other strand to attach the Lucite leaves.

**38** Attach the velvet ribbon strand. Begin by folding under one end of the velvet ribbon.

**39** With an eyelet-setting tool, set a ⅛" (2 mm) diameter eyelet in the ribbon about ⅛" (2 mm) from the fold. Trim excess ribbon from the wrong side close to the eyelet.

**40** Open an oval jump ring, insert it through the eyelet and the soldered ring on the closure, but don't close it.

**41** Arrange the ribbon across and under the other strands as desired. Smooth the strands out, straighten the closures at each end, and decide where the other end of the ribbon should be folded, adding space for a jump ring.

**42** Set an eyelet at the remaining end of the ribbon and trim excess ribbon.

**43** Open an oval jump ring, insert it through the eyelet and soldered ring, checking the length. Do not close ring.

**44** Remove the ribbon strand and set 4 more eyelets evenly spaced along its length.

**45** Gather 4 silk flowers. Trim them if they are too large for the bracelet's proportion.

**46** On a head pin, thread 1 pressed-glass spacer, one 8mm pressed-glass round bead, 1 silk flower, 1 bead cap, and 1 glass spacer or rondelle. Make a wire wrap at the top, pressing the cap down against the bead. Attach the arrangement to the ribbon using an oval jump ring on one side of an eyelet.

**47** Make and attach the rest of the flowers, alternating sides.

**48** Attach the Lucite leaves to the chain using 10mm jump rings. Add any remaining lily of the valley flowers to the bracelet as desired. I used 2 to make a dangle to hang from one corner of the buttonhole closure. I sewed 1 to the velvet ribbon and sewed 2 to the rattail cord to complete the bracelet.

## NORWEGIAN SUMMER VARIATION

Make a chic but slightly dangerous variation
with bone charms and black beads.

# Southern Belle

**FINISHED LENGTH:**
7¼" (18.5 cm)

This feminine bracelet evokes images of summer in the South: flowered cotton dresses on a hot summer day, drinking iced tea under an old oak tree with cicadas singing above, bees droning lazily over perfumed peonies. As I designed the *Southern Belle* cuff, I'd planned to let a piece of window screen play a large part. Instead, it provides a barely discernable accent, like a lace slip peeking out from the edge of a dress. If summer days and sweet tea are not to your liking, just have a few mint juleps and vamp it up with black lace, silk, and a touch of leather.

## MATERIALS

- ☐ Piece of window screen, about 3" × 3" (7.5 × 7.5 cm)
- ☐ Gilder's paste
- ☐ Makeup sponge or paper towel
- ☐ ¼ yd (23 cm) of 3" (7.5 cm) wide lace
- ☐ Small pieces of two more cotton print fabrics, about 2" × 7" (5 × 18 cm) each
- ☐ Small pieces of tulle, organza, and lace
- ☐ 1 cabochon, 18×24mm
- ☐ E6000 adhesive or Terrifically Tacky double-sided tape
- ☐ 3" × 9" (7.5 × 23 cm) beading foundation
- ☐ 5 g size 11° seed beads in one or two colors
- ☐ 6" × 9" (15 × 23 cm) cotton print fabric for cuff back
- ☐ 8 mother-of-pearl buttons, ⅜" (1 cm) diameter
- ☐ 6 mother-of-pearl buttons, ½" (1.3 cm) diameter
- ☐ 6 roses montées (sew-on rhinestones in pronged metal mount)
- ☐ 18 to 20 freshwater pearl beads
- ☐ 30 crystals in three colors, 3mm or 4mm
- ☐ 1 yd (91.5 cm) embroidery floss
- ☐ 2 snaps, size 1/0
- ☐ Beading thread of choice
- ☐ Sewing thread
- ☐ *Optional:* Beeswax to condition thread

## TOOLS

- ☐ Size 12 beading needles
- ☐ Small sharp scissors
- ☐ Utility scissors to cut window screen
- ☐ Fabric scissors
- ☐ Handsewing needle
- ☐ *Optional:* Embroidery needle

# TECHNIQUES

- Odd-count flat peyote stitch (20)
- Picot edge on peyote stitch (23)
- Sewing snaps to beadwork (44)
- Beaded cabochon with backstitch and picot edge (48)

**BEADED CABOCHON**

## STEPS

*Note: Before you get started, measure your wrist for a comfortable length for your cuff. Then add ¾" (2 cm) to that measurement for the overlap for the snaps. Our finished cuff is 7⅝" (19 cm) long. Adjust your materials measurements to achieve your desired cuff length.*

**1** Rub gilder's paste onto the piece of window screen with a makeup sponge or a paper towel. Set aside and let dry.

**2** Cut out squares and circles from the various fabrics and lace to fit diagonally on the lace, as shown in the photograph opposite.

**3** Adhere the cabochon to a piece of beading foundation and do a row of backstitch around the cabochon with size 11° seed beads, then a peyote-stitch bezel. Do another row or two of backstitch next to the bezel. With small sharp scissors, trim excess foundation, working from the wrong side. Make a picot edge around the cabochon {**FIG. 1**}.

**4** With utility scissors, cut 4 squares of window screen, each about ¾" × ¾" (2 × 2 cm). With a double thread and size 11° seed beads, edge the squares with the beads, then tie off working thread and tail threads either underneath or through the beads {**FIG. 2**}.

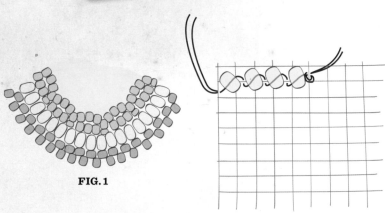

**FIG. 1**

**FIG. 2**

**5** Tear or cut the backing fabric into two strips, each about ½" (1.2 cm) narrower than the strip of lace, and slightly longer.

**6** Layer the following: lace (top), fabric (right side up next to lace), beading foundation cut ¼" (6 mm) smaller all the way around than fabric edge.

**7** Arrange the squares and circles in layers on top of the lace, with the window screen on top of the layers. With a knotted doubled sewing thread and handsewing needle, sew the layers to the lace, bringing the needle through all the layers and reinforcing well. Repeat with four groups of layered squares, circles, and window screen, leaving room in the center of the bracelet for the cabochon. Don't worry about making everything perfectly straight and even; some irregularity adds to the charm of this design.

**8** Sew on the cabochon.

**9** Sew on small pearl buttons in the angles between the fabric squares, as shown in the main photograph.

**10** Sew roses montées rhinestones along the long edges of the cuff, spaced evenly.

**11** With a doubled beading thread and size 11° seed beads, freshwater pearls, and crystals, stitch a random vine pattern meandering over the cuff, as desired. Tie off thread. Bring the needle through the layers to secure. Bring the needle up near or beside the last bead.

**12** With small sharp scissors, trim the ends of the beading foundation if necessary.

**13** Put the second piece of cotton backing fabric right side down over the beading

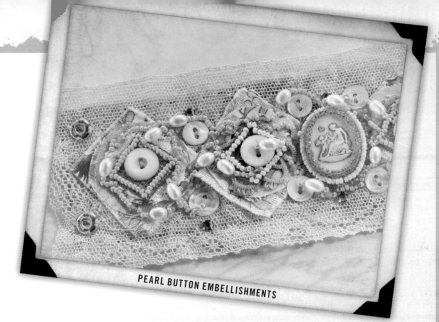

**PEARL BUTTON EMBELLISHMENTS**

foundation. Tuck the ends of both cotton strips under. With a handsewing needle and two strands of embroidery floss, blanket stitch or whipstitch the fabric ends together.

**14** Continue using the embroidery floss to stitch a running stitch along one edge, right at the edge of the foundation, sewing through the cotton layers only. Tie off thread when you are close to the other end.

**15** Begin stitching in running stitch with two strands of embroidery floss at the end where you first turned under the edges. Stitch along the edge. When you're close to the end, turn under the cotton fabric edges and whipstitch or blanket-stitch along the edge. Use a running stitch to meet where you left off. Tie off thread.

**16** Sew on 2 size 1/0 snaps at one end of the cuff.

**17** Sew the other halves of the snaps to the other end of the cuff, on the wrong side. On the right side, sew 2 pearl buttons over the snaps to keep the lace flat and to complete the cuff.

# → Conclusion

**SO YOU'VE THOROUGHLY RAIDED YOUR JEWELRY BOX,** hit the local antiques shops and weekend yard sales, and accumulated a wonderful array of objects. You've learned some of the techniques in this book, experimented with the projects, and come up with a few tricks of your own.

It's time now to take these new experiences and start out on your own creative journey. It is my hope that you have become more aware of the myriad objects around you, and that things you might have walked past without a second glance—the worn, broken, and cast-off detritus of life—now ignite your imagination.

If you're at all like me, images whirl about in your mind like brightly colored fall leaves as you envision all the ways you can use these newly discovered treasures. As you hold each object in your hand and feel its history, may you find endless and exciting ways to not only tell its story but your own.

*Melanie Doerman*

*The Story Pendant, page 64*

# → Resources

**TO FIND UNCONVENTIONAL OBJECTS** for my mixed-media beadweaving and jewelry making, I shop everywhere from flea markets and antiques stores to local bead shops and mainstream craft and hobby stores. I also scour the Internet. Secondhand stores, flea markets, and online auctions such as ebay.com are good for objects such as chandelier parts, keyhole findings, watches and watchcases, antique shoe buckles, and vintage photographs and ephemera. Try hardware stores for window screen, carpet tape, and galvanized washers.

## MISCELLANEOUS OBJECTS AND TRIMS

**Butterfly Utopia**
butterflyutopia.com
*Downloadable butterfly images*

**Gilding the Lily Vintage**
gildingthelilyvintage.blogspot.com
*Eiffel Tower souvenir charms*

**Kabela Design**
kabeladesign.com
*Filigree, gilder's paste, charms*

**M&J Trimming**
mjtrim.com
*Ribbons, rhinestones, buttons*

**Ornamentea**
ornamentea.com
*Hannah silk cord, beads*

**Serendipity Salvage**
etsy.com/shop/serendipitysalvage
*Small bottles, ephemera, reverse-painted glass cabochons*

**Susan Clarke Originals**
susanclarkeoriginals.com
*Unusual buttons*

**Stamp Francisco**
stampfrancisco.com
*Dragonfly-wing rubber stamps*

**Stampin' Up**
stampinup.com
*Crop-a-Dile eyelet-setting tool, embellishments, stamps*

**The Doll House Elora**
eloradollhouse.com
*Porcelain doll hands*

**The Magpie**
themagpie.com
*Author's website; Frozen Charlotte doll in plastic box available for sale*

**Tim Holtz**
timholtz.com
*Keyhole findings and other mixed-media products*

**Timeless Trims**
timelesstrims.com
*Antique and vintage trims and ribbons*

**Vintage Jewelry Supplies**
vintagejewelrysupplies.com
*Brass filigree*

## BEADS AND FINDINGS

**Artbeads.com**
artbeads.com
*Rubber cord, beads, findings*

**Beadology**
beadology.net
*Lucite leaves, beads*

**Bella Finding House**
bellafindings.com
*Beads and findings*

**Berger Specialty Co.**
bergerbeads.net
*Beads and beading supplies*

**Caravan Beads**
caravanbeads.com
*Large selection of seed beads*

## BEADS AND FINDINGS, CONT.

**Earthly Adornments**
earthlyadornments.com
*Vintage cabochons, beads, and jewelry*

**Garden of Beaden**
gardenofbeadenupland.com
*Beads and supplies*

**Kandras Beads**
kandrasbeads.com
*Seed beads*

**Lisa Kan Designs**
lisakan.com
*Caged bead caps*

**The San Gabriel Bead Company**
beadcompany.com
*Beads and supplies in Arcadia, California*

## GENERAL ART AND MIXED-MEDIA SUPPLIES

**Art Supply Warehouse**
aswexpress.com
*General art and craft supplies*

**eBay**
ebay.com
*Worldwide online auction house*

**Etsy**
etsy.com
*Supplies for crafting and handmade items*

**Interweave Store**
interweavestore.com
*Mixed-media, art, and craft supplies*

**Michael's Arts & Crafts**
michaels.com
*General art and craft supplies*

FAIRY SHRINE, PAGE 108

# ➙Recommended Reading

Alexander, Sally Jean. *Pretty Little Things: Collage Jewelry, Trinkets, Keepsakes.* Cincinnati, Ohio: North Light Books, 2006.

Cannarella, Deborah. *Beading for the Soul: Inspired Designs from 23 Contemporary Artists.* Loveland, Colorado: Interweave, 2005.

Cook, Jeannette, and Vicki Star. *Beading with Peyote Stitch: A Beadwork How-To Book.* Loveland, Colorado: Interweave, 2000.

Cypher, Carol Huber. *Mastering Beadwork: A Comprehensive Guide to Off-Loom Techniques.* Loveland, Colorado: Interweave, 2007.

Deeb, Margie. *The Beader's Guide to Color.* New York: Potter Craft, 2004.

Hector, Valerie. *The Art of Beadwork: Historic Inspiration, Contemporary Design.* New York: Potter Craft, 2005.

Kan, Lisa. *Bead Romantique: Elegant Beadweaving Designs.* Loveland, Colorado: Interweave, 2007.

Lee, Stephanie. *Semiprecious Salvage: Creating Found-Art Jewelry.* Cincinnati, Ohio: North Light Books, 2008.

Prussing, Christine. *Beading with Right Angle Weave: A Beadwork How-To Book.* Loveland, Colorado: Interweave, 2004.

Sersich, Stephanie. *Designing Jewelry with Glass Beads.* Loveland, Colorado: Interweave, 2008.

Snelling, Kelly, and Ruth Rae. *A Charming Exchange: 25 Jewelry Projects to Create & Share.* Cincinnati, Ohio: North Light Books, 2008.

Thornton, Cynthia. *Enchanted Adornments: Creating Mixed-Media Jewelry with Metal Clay, Wire, Resin & More.* Loveland, Colorado: Interweave, 2009.

Wells, Carol Wilcox. *Creative Bead Weaving: A Contemporary Guide to Classic Off-Loom Stitches.* Asheville, North Carolina: Lark Books, 1998.

# → Index

beads 10

cabochon, beaded 48--51
chain-nose pliers 13
clasp, ribbon strap 54–55
conditioners, thread 11
Crop-A-Dile tool 13
cranky wire wrap 41
crystals 10
cutters, flush 13; thread 12; X-Acto 13; wire 13

decreases 22, 26, 28
Dremel tool 13
drill 13

edge, picot 23, 51
embellishment 30–31
even-count tubular peyote stitch 25
eyelet setter 13

fabric, foundation 12
file 13
flat-nose pliers 13
foiling 42–43
found objects 16–17
fringe, beaded 35

gilder's paste 13
glue 13

increases 26, 27

joining peyote stitch to right-angle weave 32–33
journaling 98–99
jump ring, opening and closing 41

ladder stitch 34
link, ribbon 52–53

machine, sewing 13

needles, beading 11
netting, tubular 36–37

odd-count flat peyote stitch 20–22

pass back through 21
pass through 21
paste, gilder's 13
peyote stitch 20–29, 32
pliers 13
punch 13

resin 13
right-angle weave 30  33
rope, spiral 38–39
round-nose pliers 13

scissors 13
seed beads 10
snaps, sewing 44–45
spiral rope 38–39
stitch in the ditch 29

tape, double-sided 13
thimble, beaded 46–47
thread 11; adding 86; tying off 86
thread conditioners 11
thread cutters 12
tube shape, zipping 24
tubular netting 36–37

wire 12
wireworking tools 12–13
wire wrapping 40–41
work space 81

X-Acto knife 13